God of
 All Promises

Visit www.wjkbooks.com/Promises to download a free book club guide for group discussion and individual reflection.

Other recent books by Walter Brueggemann

Prayer books:

Waiting in Gratitude: Prayers of Joy

Following into Risky Obedience: Prayers along the Journey

Acting in the Wake: Prayers for Justice

Individual studies/devotionals:

Journey to the Common Good, Updated Edition

Gift and Task: A Year of Daily Readings and Reflections

Group studies:

Materiality as Resistance: Five Elements for Moral Action in the Real World

From Judgment to Hope: A Study on the Prophets

Interrupting Silence: God's Command to Speak Out

Sabbath as Resistance: Saying No to the Culture of Now, New Edition with Study Guide

"Walter Brueggemann's *God of All Promises* provides a devotional lens to explore the book of beginnings. Intentionally theological, these reflections model a way for us to, in his words, 'pray back' to the text. Moreover, the poetic form of each entry reminds us of the ways in which the Bible is inherently poetic, dialogical, and invitational, calling us into a space where we can be challenged, surprised, delighted, sometimes troubled, but always transformed. This is a great resource for individual and group study."

—Judy Fentress-Williams, Dodge Professor of Biblical Interpretation, Virginia Theological Seminary

"What a tremendous gift the late Walter Brueggemann has bequeathed to the church. His poetic and prayerful reflections on each chapter of Genesis are insightful, heartfelt, and profoundly edifying. In these pages, Brueggemann models a way of engaging Scripture that makes it come alive—opening its divine wisdom and revealing its deep relevance for our lives today. I wholeheartedly recommend *God of All Promises* to all who love Scripture and to any who long to love Scripture but aren't yet sure how."

—Greg Boyd, Senior Pastor, Woodland Hills Church

"Brueggemann powerfully and elegantly crafts insights into Genesis. His poetic words draw us in and shake us up. He reminds us that faith's peculiar language shall form our reflections and deepen our prayers, if we let it. This book is a beautiful companion to his beloved *Genesis* commentary!"

—Clover Reuter Beal, Co-pastor, Montview Boulevard Presbyterian Church

"Forty-three years ago, Brueggemann published his robust commentary on Genesis. Now, toward the end of his life, he has returned to Genesis with the fresh eyes of a poet, 'praying back' the text to God. Brueggemann offers a prayerful way of living into the text, and we receive it as his parting gift."
— William P. Brown, William Marcellus McPheeters Professor of Old Testament, Columbia Theological Seminary

"This rich collection testifies to Brueggemann's abiding love of the Hebrew Scriptures and his wisdom about spiritual formation. His expositions of Genesis texts are saturated with poetic drama, theological depth, and ethical honesty. This book is beautifully suited for Bible studies, devotional reading, and discussion groups eager to link biblical theology with contemporary issues."
— Carolyn J. Sharp, Professor of Homiletics, Yale Divinity School

"In these pages, Brueggemann helps us hear Genesis again with wonder and honesty. His poetic prayers slow us down long enough to notice a God who keeps creating, calling, and promising right in the middle of our disorder. This book is a companion for anyone who wants Scripture to shape not just their thinking but their hope."
— Josh Kingcade, Senior Minister, Preston Road Church of Christ

"A devotional, a prayer book, an intimate reflection on the deep stories of our faith in conversation with the God we meet in Genesis: a gift. Read this as a pastor preparing to preach on these texts, read this as liturgy in worship as a prayer of the people, read this as a person of faith longing to connect with the God that sometimes seems so strange and yet so wonderful in these ancient stories. Brueggemann spans the distance between ancient and present, speaking words on our behalf that connect us as a family of faith across the generations. Above all, this book testifies to Brueggemann's life work as a biblical scholar: an act of faith seeking understanding, to both obey and plead with the God we meet in Scripture."

— Carolyn B. Helsel, Associate Professor
in the Blair Monie Distinguished Chair
in Homiletics, Austin Seminary

"These 'prayers and probes' have been inspired by one last reading through the book of Genesis by a master exegete, who, as it turns out, is also a master poet. How appropriate! This little book is a treasure, left to us unexpectedly by one who has taught us much. And in this last contribution, he continues teaching. One can almost hear his voice when reading these prayers, like one following Professor Brueggemann on a poetic pilgrimage one last time through the text he loved so well."

— Bill T. Arnold, Paul S. Amos Professor
of Old Testament Interpretation,
Asbury Theological Seminary

God of All Promises

A Poetic Pilgrimage through Genesis

WALTER BRUEGGEMANN

© 2026 Walter Brueggemann
Suggestions for Reading © 2026
Westminster John Knox Press

First edition
Published by Westminster John Knox Press
Louisville, Kentucky

26 27 28 29 30 31 32 33 34 35—10 9 8 7 6 5 4 3 2 1

All rights reserved. No part of this book may be reproduced or transmitted in any form or by any means, electronic or mechanical, including photocopying, recording, or by any information storage or retrieval system, without permission in writing from the publisher. For information, address Westminster John Knox Press, 100 Witherspoon Street, Louisville, Kentucky 40202-1396. Or contact us online at www.wjkbooks.com.

Unless otherwise indicated, Scripture quotations are from the New Revised Standard Version of the Bible, copyright © 1989 by the Division of Christian Education of the National Council of the Churches of Christ in the U.S.A., and are used by permission.

Book design by Drew Stevens
Cover design by Geronna Lewis-Lyte

Library of Congress Cataloging-in-Publication Data is on file
at the Library of Congress, Washington, DC.

ISBN: 978-0-664-26938-8 (paperback)
ISBN: 978-1-646-98449-7 (ebook)

Most Westminster John Knox Press books are available at special quantity discounts when purchased in bulk by corporations, organizations, and special-interest groups. For more information, please e-mail SpecialSales@wjkbooks.com.

*In remembrance of
Allen G. Wehrli,
my first teacher in the book of Genesis*

CONTENTS

Preface: Prayers and Probes	xi
Suggestions for Reading	xv
On Reading Genesis 1	1
On Reading Genesis 2	3
On Reading Genesis 3	5
On Reading Genesis 4	7
On Reading Genesis 5	9
On Reading Genesis 6	12
On Reading Genesis 7	15
On Reading Genesis 8	18
On Reading Genesis 9	21
On Reading Genesis 10	25
On Reading Genesis 11	29
On Reading Genesis 12	32
On Reading Genesis 13	34
On Reading Genesis 14	37
On Reading Genesis 15	39
On Reading Genesis 16	41
On Reading Genesis 17	45
On Reading Genesis 18	48

On Reading Genesis 19	52
On Reading Genesis 20	55
On Reading Genesis 21	57
On Reading Genesis 22	61
On Reading Genesis 23	65
On Reading Genesis 24	68
On Reading Genesis 25	72
On Reading Genesis 26	76
On Reading Genesis 27	79
On Reading Genesis 28	83
On Reading Genesis 29	87
On Reading Genesis 30	91
On Reading Genesis 31	96
On Reading Genesis 32	100
On Reading Genesis 33	104
On Reading Genesis 34	108
On Reading Genesis 35	112
On Reading Genesis 36	114
On Reading Genesis 37	117
On Reading Genesis 38	121
On Reading Genesis 39	124
On Reading Genesis 40	127
On Reading Genesis 41	129
On Reading Genesis 42	133
On Reading Genesis 43	137
On Reading Genesis 44	141
On Reading Genesis 45	144

On Reading Genesis 46	148
On Reading Genesis 47	151
On Reading Genesis 48	155
On Reading Genesis 49	159
On Reading Genesis 50	163
Conclusion: Beyond the Ancestors	167
Other Prayers Addressed to the Same Holy Listener	
A Prayer: You Three Times Holy	171
A Prayer: Your Cosmic Pledge of Disarmament	174
A Prayer: You with the Long Nose	176
A Prayer: Fresh from the Word	179

PREFACE: PRAYERS AND PROBES

When I began work on this manuscript, I had in mind only to compose prayers in response to the specificity of the text. I have found it possible and useful, in my own practice, to pray back the Bible to the God who dwells therein. I soon discovered, however, that there are texts in the book of Genesis that do not lend themselves readily to pray back. For that reason, I have added probes—critical reflections—alongside prayers and meditations. Thus, in some texts in the book of Genesis, I have offered a probe into the plot or the characters of texts or into the way in which narrative art performs in the texts. Probes allow me to push and poke and tease the text in order to see what it may yield to such insistence. I have not made a sharp distinction between prayers and probes in each chapter because I believe that both are exercises in engagement with the text, with the God of the text, and with the people who live in and from the text.

Two features of my exposition may be noted. First, I have attempted a more or less poetic rendering of my response to the text. I have done so in order to reflect the deliberate elusiveness of the text that invites us to pause as we read. In that pause,

- we may engage in critical reflection on the text,
- we may engage in appreciation of the art form of the text, or
- we may take the text as a script for prayer and meditation.

I have intended to provide ample space for the reader to exercise freedom with the text and to let that freedom be in the service of our common growth in faith.

The reader will notice, second, that I have concluded each exposition with a brief closing prayer and an "amen." Such an ending, of course, reflects our common usage about prayer. But where I have done a probe rather than a prayer in the exposition, I have also used the "amen" in order to assent, as fully as I can, to the instruction of the text as I have understood it. Where such an assent does not ring true for the reader, it can be safely disregarded.

It is, of course, commonly recognized that the book of Genesis falls into two unequal parts:

- a rendering of the world in chapters 1–11, and
- a rendering of the chosen family in chapters 12–50.

The two parts are linked in the text by the assertion of God's blessing, most especially God's blessing to Abraham. That blessing has on its horizon all the families of the earth, thus humanity beyond the scope of Abraham's own family. We may take that reference to "all the families of the earth" (Gen. 12:3) with reference to the fulsome genealogy of Genesis 10.

This twofold articulation of the reach of God's good governance in both realms is echoed in the statement of faith of my own church, the United Church of Christ. That statement (that has official standing but no normative insistence) voices the call of God in a way not unlike the two parts of the book of Genesis:

- God calls the worlds into being;
- God calls us into the church.

These two formulations together affirm the call and work of God both in creation and in the more specific community of faith.

When I think about a poetic engagement with the book of Genesis, I most gladly call to mind the poetic iteration of the early chapters of Genesis by B. Davie Napier in his wondrous rendering *Come Sweet Death: A Quintet from Genesis* (Pilgrim Press, 1981). I was able to hear Napier read his moving rhetoric at Eden Theological Seminary as the work was being published. In any case, I pause to salute Napier for his earlier book *From Faith to Faith: Essays on Old Testament Literature* (Harper & Brothers, 1955). I read that book as a middler at Eden Seminary; it provided for me a major impetus for my decision to pursue Old Testament study, a decision I have never regretted. As I recall, Napier's book is an early English-language probe from the work of Gerhard von Rad that had not yet reached English translation.

I am glad to dedicate this book to the memory of Allen G. Wehrli, my first Old Testament teacher. Wehrli had studied at the University of Halle under Hermann Gunkel. He had, like

Gunkel, a deep interest in the way narrative functioned in the Bible and in particular in the book of Genesis. In my first semester of Old Testament introduction with Wehrli, in my junior year in seminary, he regaled us with his well-told biblical narratives. But he deceived us. We thought he was just telling stories that he rendered as an art form. Only later in graduate school did I discover that he had presented to us Gunkel's complete taxonomy of the narrative Gattungen (genres) in the Bible. Wehrli was also my first teacher of Hebrew, and he managed us with uncommon patience. As I studied with him later in his years of teaching, so also was my father his student at Eden Seminary in Wehrli's early years of teaching. In some formal way I was appointed as his successor in the faculty of Eden Seminary, but he was in truth a master teacher who had among us no real successor. (I am glad to say that his learned son, Eugene Wehrli, was also my teacher and then my colleague, neighbor, and friend, who eventually became the president of Eden Seminary.) No doubt the church lives by the benefit of such teachers who bless our lives with their learning, their passion, and their cunning faithfulness. My debt to Allen Wehrli is immense and continuing.

It is my hope that these brief expositions will serve the church well in the nurture of our common faith with energy and courage for our common ministry.

Walter Brueggemann

SUGGESTIONS FOR READING

These poetic and prayerful meditations on each chapter of Genesis draw on Walter Brueggemann's enduring faith, cultivated over a lifetime of study and love for the Scriptures. Each reflection brings together theological and devotional insight in the form of a poem, crafted to offer readers deep anchors for their own faith. Brueggemann's inquisitive explorations wrestle with the text and with both the grace and failings of our humanity, drawing out the themes of God's persistent, loving purpose in the midst of our beautiful and troubled worlds, then and now.

You may choose to engage these reflections in a few different ways. They can be used for individual devotion and study or in a group setting. It is helpful to read the poems alongside the text of Genesis, whether before, after, or interspersed with the reflections—whatever helps to illuminate your experience of the biblical text. For group discussion, you could meet weekly and discuss a few chapters at each session or hold a longer study if you wish to cover one chapter per week. You may also consider responding creatively as you read, individually or as a group, by journaling, writing your own poetic interpretations, or engaging imaginatively through painting, drawing, sculpting with clay, making a collage, or whatever creative approach you would like. Each poem opens with a thematic epigraph from Scripture and ends with a closing prayer to deepen reflection and guide your devotional and study time. Visit www.wjkbooks.com/Promises to download a free book club guide for group discussion and individual reflection.

The foundational stories of the families of faith in Genesis are rich, strange, troubling, and inspiring. With Brueggemann as our guide, we can see how God's good governance, faithfulness, love, and care have continually formed God's people to be a blessing to all, summoning us beyond strife and grief into God's audacious, holy promises.

ON READING GENESIS 1

When you send forth your spirit, they are created;
and you renew the face of the ground.
(Ps. 104:30)

At the outset there was you;
   only you in your majestic splendor;
   only you ready in your generative love.
And then from you
   heaven and earth as your domains,
   night and darkness as your zones of governance,
   chaos turned to ordered life.
You loved the world
   stooping down to evoke plants: corn, petunias, poison ivy;
   bending low in your gentle summons to animals: kangaroos, rabbits, alligators;
   reaching in, you dreamed the fish: lobsters, catfish, and tiny minnows.
You did not quit your work until you came to us;
   when you blessed;
   when you blessed in our gender identity;
   when you gave authority to manage the earth,
      to preside over plants with care,
      to host your animals with attentiveness,
      to protect your water creatures great and small.
You blessed them; you blessed us;
you saw that it was good; your words are "Very good!"
And then you rested, enough work, enough
creating, enough presiding over newness!

And we — we receive your blessing of mercy;
>   we breathe in your breath of life;
>   we receive your teeming world of creatureliness;
>   we receive the power to care for it . . . or not;
>   we receive your permit to rest as you rest.

We pledge before you that we will accept our creatureliness from you
>   with its freedom;
>   with its authority;
>   with its responsibility.

We will manage so that the other creatures can see your image,
>   in seeing us at our best.

We praise and thank and bless you . . . only you . . . you alone.

> *Giver of life abundant, we are on the receiving end of your dazzling gifts.*
> *We receive your gifts gladly and are grateful for your good generosity.*
> *We are glad to be among your many well-beloved creatures. Amen.*

ON READING GENESIS 2

Therefore a man leaves his father and his mother and clings to his wife, and they become one flesh.

(Gen. 2:24)

How great thou art!
You breathed out your power and vitality.
You blew your life-giving breath on our skeletal structure.
   Our bones received your vitality and we became alive
     to you and
     to the world.
You in your lordly authority give us work to do;
   you reach us with only two words:
     to *serve* the garden of delight,
     to *keep* the plantings of life,
   to serve and to keep, a strange notion of dominion!
   You give us the work of prospering the whole of creation.
   In that moment we become responsible for the health of all creation.
You give us dominion,
   freedom to manage creation,
   a capacity to name and touch the other creatures,
   the burden of cherishing creation.
You give us companions,
   a woman for a man,
   a man for a woman,
   a lover for a lover.

We begin our new life
> with power, vitality, well-being, authority, energy.

We are before you;

We are in the world;

We are unhindered; our lives are unhindered in work, in freedom, in companionship.

We gladly accept our vocation as your agents of blessing.
> Because of us, the world has a chance for well-being.

We bask in your greatness;
> We celebrate the good work you give us;
> We rejoice in the life you make possible
>> as we stand as sign of your good governance.

You are the God of companionship, and you will us to live in trusting relationships.

For good, trustworthy companions who sustain us day by day, we give you thanks.

We take their fidelity to us as an expression of your durable loyalty to us. Amen.

ON READING GENESIS 3

"Father, I have sinned against heaven and before you;
I am no longer worthy to be called your son."
(Luke 15:18–19)

There was a whisperer in the garden of delight.
    It was an inexplicable *hiss* that pursued us day and night.
    It whispered counter-thoughts to us,
        pushing us outside our easy innocence.
The voice of whisper made us double-minded:
    we intended to do the work God gave us to do;
    at the same time we now thought otherwise.
    We wondered if we had to do the work.
    We reasoned that we were entitled to more than that.
    We had wants and desires beyond God that seemed to us like needs.
We gave in to our wondering eyes,
        to our greedy hearts,
        to our untamed appetites.
In an instant of such unwarranted self-assertion,
    we felt a new sense that Freud would term "shame."
    We knew a deep embarrassment that Luther would call "guilt."
The very God who loved us into being came seeking us.
    We, in our embarrassment, hid, hoping to conceal ourselves.
    We blamed each other; we blamed the whisperer.
    We made every excuse we could imagine.

But none persuaded him. He fated us to a harder life.
He left us vulnerable, exposed, driven, displaced.
At that last moment, he clothed us in protection.
> But still we were on the outs, excluded by our choices,
>
> We forfeited the innocence that had been a gift we now threw away.

In that moment we discovered that the giver of all good gifts was more than just kind.
The God who summoned the earth had a gritty purpose.
Our violation of that gritty purpose has left us on edge, on guard, endlessly at risk.
We may have known better, but we refused and blew it.
> And now here we are!

You, Lord of our families, must ache as we ache when we know of the fractures in our most treasured relationships and when we notice the violence among the nations. In your ache restore us to the well-being of your good purposes. Amen.

ON READING GENESIS 4

*How very good and pleasant it is
when kindred live together in unity!
(Ps. 133:1)*

Before tribe, before nation-state, before empire,
   there was the nuclear family.
God intended that family of sisters and brothers to
dwell in unity.
Mostly we do not!
   Mostly sisters and brothers dwell in uneasy rivalry,
      competing for love, or honor, or attention, or
         property,
     competing
       sometimes in legal action;
       often in verbal abuse;
       occasionally in physical violence.
Brothers become adversaries,
   sisters become competitors,
     siblings become rivals, all after the same benefits.
And then violence:
   violence of Whites against brothers and sisters of
     color;
   violence of Israelis against Palestinian sisters and
     brothers . . . and vice versa;
   violence of clans and tribes and nation-states,
   violence unending, uncurbed, undisciplined,
     unlimited.
And then we are asked:
   Where is your brother?
   How is your sister?

We find ourselves accountable, having to give answer,
- for long generations of violence,
- for greedy practices of usurpation,
- for the ugly disposal of siblings.

Mostly we ignore the question asked by the Lord of our family.
Mostly we keep busy, avert our eyes, and pretend we did not hear.
> But late, in the quiet, we know we must give answer,
> - too late for forgiveness,
> - too soon for restoration,
> - too heavy for bearing.

And so we live in a world of vengeance;
- the killing must go on;
- the violence must continue;
- the bloodletting is endless.

We wish we were numb to it;
- except that the question penetrates our defense and our denial:
- where is your sister?
- how goes it with your brother?

We spend our days brooding in resistance in a remote land.

Either that, or we join the party, welcoming the long-lost sibling into the family, the inheritance, and the well-being.

That either-or pursues, no matter where we flee.

We know that we cannot love you whom we have not seen when we do not love our brother and sister whom we see. Give us generosity of spirit that we may overcome our alienations, and live in well-being with our siblings, even those so unlike us. Amen.

ON READING GENESIS 5

I am reminded of your sincere faith,
a faith that lived first in your grandmother Lois and your mother Eunice
and now, I am sure, lives in you.

(2 Tim. 1:5)

We come from a long line. That long line stretches way, way back,
   back behind our memory,
   back behind any record,
   back behind any traceable genealogy,
     all the way back, back to the beginning.
That long linkage is filled out by many characters playing many roles.
   No doubt those many characters in many roles
     continue to be operative through us,
     continue to be roles we may adopt,
     continue to be characters we may reperform.
   We have many options from that long linkage.
Among them is "the image of God,"
   for all those in the linkage, "the image of God"
     has been
   insistent,
     indelible,
       unending,
"image of God" loaded with power, authority, generativity, and responsibility.
We may choose otherwise, but the image persists.
Perhaps every family has somewhere in its memory an Enoch—

who walked with God,
who embodied grace and dignity,
who performed godlike generativity and generosity.
We remember Enoch among us so good and so wise
that he never died but was "taken."
We could choose to reperform this Enoch, walking with God.
Or we notice that our line runs toward Noah,
Noah *(noah)* who brought us "relief" *(nhm)*.
He relieved our family from worry, vexation, and hard labor.
We could be yet another Enoch in our linkage, "walking with God."
Or we could be yet another Noah, bringing relief to our long family.
Or mostly we could join the long line of the almost forgotten,
for whom the story is not more than "lived . . . died . . . forgotten."

We are always choosing our family role,
our peculiar assignment,
our place in the genealogy.
However we choose, we share the identity.
We carry the blessing.
We have life from the God who created us, every one of us,
the crooks, the healers, the lowlifes, the blessers, the slobs.
It is a long line, and we belong in it,
with a chance to turn toward the blessing giver and receive.

*God of our years and our generations,
God of our memories and our hopes,
we pray for your gifts of sustenance and steadfastness
that we may walk in the ways of faith,
bring glory to you,
and well-being to our earth. Amen.*

ON READING GENESIS 6

> *For whenever I speak, I must cry out,*
> *I must shout, "Violence and destruction!"*
> *For the word of the LORD has become for me*
> *a reproach and derision all day long.*
> *(Jer. 20:8)*

Our verses begin with "evil."
That "evil," it is said, is deep in the human heart,
> so deep that everything is skewed,
> so deep that the creator God is driven to regret.

That regret is so heavy that the creator God thinks to do extermination.
> Imagine! A God bent on genocide of God's own creation!

There is a footnote that interrupts this sorry scene.
> The footnote is of Noah,
>> the one who contradicts the sorry business of evil,
>> the one who evokes God's special, seeming arbitrary notice.

We cling to this footnote, a slight way of escape from our sorry history of evil.

The evil that God sees issues in violence.
> We know that story well:
>> We participate in that tale of violence;
>> We keep the narrative of hate open-ended in our own lives.

The God who watches as evil becomes violence is moved to counterviolence,
> enough to destroy the evil-doers and the earth.

This show of holiness shocks us.
   We are accustomed to God's
      love,
         mercy,
           compassion,
             kindness,
               gentleness . . .
   and now a resolve to destroy!
This creator God—one so vexed by the failure of creation,
   can operate on a dual track:
      ready to destroy and exterminate;
      attentive to the good family of Noah,
         the one exceptional in God's favor,
         the one excepted from God's punishment.

We remember that our long family line stretched to Noah
   on whom our future depends,
   as does the future of all creation.
We are grateful that God's outrage allowed room for an exception.
   God provided an ark of rescue,
      a boat of safety and survival.
   God specified cubits and cypress wood and three decks.
   God protected every species of animal, bird, creeping thing,
      a boatload of beloved creatures.
It is enough for us to sing,
   "Be not dismayed whate'er betide,
   God will take care of you."
      God will provide a safety net for this family,

God will provide food and buoyancy
> a blessed life outside the destruction.

The storyteller holds Noah up as a choice recipient of God's attentive care:
> Noah as the wave of the future,
> Noah as the one who brings relief, whose name means "rest,"
> a model of obedience,
> the singular partner with God in covenant.

The story of violence does not retreat;
the story of divine rejection does not compromise.
But the story of violence and divine rejection is not the true story.
The true story is of Noah, the one aligned with God.
> The old, old story is one of violence and anger;
> Noah is the subject of the new, new song, the song concerning God's future.

We are left with an uncompromising either-or:
> either to join the crowd in its violence
> or to embrace the covenant of obedience.

The choice is a very old one and as urgent as our life today.

Amid our troubled world we give you thanks, O God,
for that faithful company of your people who keep watch,
who tell the truth, and
who continue to act out your good purposes.
Strengthen and sustain those agents of good and keep them in your attentive care. Amen.

ON READING GENESIS 7

The earth was a formless void and darkness covered the face of
   the deep,
while a wind from God swept over the face of the waters.

(Gen. 1:2)

The ark was filled with two of every kind;
   but the "purity cops" intruded into the story—
   now it is some "clean," some "unclean,"
   some welcome, some a threat . . . all sorted out!
Then rain came on all of them.
   The rain came mightily;
      The fountains of the great deep burst forth. . . .
      The waters swelled and increased. . . .
      The windows of the heavens were opened,
         so mightily that they covered the mountains.
The waters, we do not doubt, are a show of God's power.
   The creator God commands the waters.
      The God of mighty waters evokes our stunned
         Joban doxology:
   "Who has cut a channel for the torrents of rain,
      and a way for the thunderbolt,
   to bring rain on a land where no one lives,
      on the desert, which is empty of human life,
   to satisfy the waste and desolate land,
      and to make the ground put forth grass?

   "Has the rain a father,
      or who has begotten the drops of dew?

> From whose womb did the ice come forth,
>> and who has given birth to the hoarfrost of heaven?
> The waters become hard like stone,
>> and the face of the deep is frozen." (Job 38:25–30)

We know the answer.
> This is the God who sets limits on the rage of chaos: "Thus far and no farther."
> This is the God who unleashed the waters to drown Pharaoh, his chariots, and his horses.
> This is the God who dried the Jordan so that Joshua could cross it.
> Water is a creature of God's good purpose,
> Water is a source of wonder that exhibits God's governance.
>> And so it rained and rained and rained and rained.

We watched from the ark. In the end, only Noah and his family survived,
> saved by the ark, the one God had provided.

It was a long rain, some said forty days;
>> others said it was 150 days.
>>> Either way, the boat stayed dry and above the waves.
>>>> We watched the mighty power of God.
>>>> We observed God's assault on violence.
>>>> We saw God's governance come to the recalcitrant.

We were glad to be in the boat of covenant promises.
It turned out, *beyond our understanding,*
> that the faithful God of covenant is the mighty Lord of creation.

It was for us a moment of awe and recognition;
> It was an occasion for gratitude and for worship.
>> It was a scene of many deaths,
>>> with only those rescued by God for life preserved for covenant.

We pause, when we remember, in gratitude and wonder. We know, in our own lives, something of the dark threat of chaotic waters. We nonetheless trust that you hold the world in your hands, that your good care overrides the threats that put us at risk. We are glad for your reliable, faithful governance of the world that comes at us in such disordered ways. Amen.

ON READING GENESIS 8

He woke up and rebuked the wind, and said to the sea, "Peace! Be still!" Then the wind ceased.

(Mark 4:39)

The "blotting" out of destruction was as though God
>had gone crazy,
>had lost God's mind,
>had forgotten creation was a treasure to be loved.

And then—abruptly, God remembered!
>God remembered Noah and the boatload of protected species.

When God remembered,
>the rush of the storm was suddenly reversed.
>Now God's drying wind blew.
>Now God's rain stopped.

Now God's mighty waters receded to their proper place.
The scene of drying out was long and slow.
>But it did happen,
>when the Holy One was spent in anger,
>now restored to sanity as creator.

God released his safe passengers to bask in God's good governance,
>—all of them, Noah, his wife, his sons, their wives, birds, animals, creeping things.
>It was a moment like that of the initial creation.
>It was creation beginning again, after the drastic purging.

In that moment God arrived at new clarity:
>at the outset God had seen the "evil inclination" of the human heart.

Now, post-flood, God again acknowledges the "evil inclination" of the human heart.
Nothing has changed: the human heart remained hard and recalcitrant and unheeding.
But then everything was now different . . . because God had changed.
The God of angry destructiveness now becomes the God of covenantal fidelity.
God is now with a new resolve:
> Never again!
> Never again such anger!
> Never again such wholesale destruction!
> Never again destroying the world God made and loves.

"Never again" becomes a passion for God,
> from which may come new futures,
> because God declares a steady, reliable, life-giving order:

Seed time and
> harvest,
>> cold and
>>> heat,
>>>> summer and
>>>>> winter,
>>>>>> day and
>>>>>>> night!

Never to cease!
That divine declaration, when we recall it, leaves us speechless in wonder.
> We are not ready for divine wrath to become divine fidelity.
> But then it was; we knew it.

We did not doubt it;
> we knew that after the flood we could begin again,
> > falling back on God's assured blessing.

The scar of the flood is everywhere.
> We can see it in the savaged land;
> we sense it in bruised humanity;
> we spot it in God's own life,
>
> a scar by which we remember our own failed life.

And then we are jarred by the chant of reliability:
> Seedtime, harvest, cold, heat, summer, winter, day, night!

No more deathly intrusions from the God of all faithfulness.

It is a hard-won assurance, now on the lips of the creator.

> *We know about the storm. We know about the chaotic waters. But we also know of your good governance. We know that you, creator God, still the storms, cast out demons, and quiet the force of evil. We know and do not doubt. We pray for your attentiveness to our world so deeply under threat. Do your lordly quieting work; give us peace beyond the fearful chaos. Amen.*

ON READING GENESIS 9

> *I did not say to the offspring of Jacob,*
> *"Seek me in chaos."*
> *I the LORD speak the truth,*
> *I declare what is right.*
>
> *(Isa. 45:19)*

Post-flood was such a wondrous time of restoration!
> God was on best behavior!
> Bygones are bygones!

Now begins a new blessing from God. Noah and his family received new blessing,
> the same one as uttered in the ancient garden of creation.

The whole of creation is mobilized for human well-being.
> There is, we note well, a lingering footnote:
> "Do not shed blood!"
> The one you may want to kill is made in God's own image, entitled to life.

The blessing leads to covenant.
> The covenant is with Noah and his family.
> The covenant is with every living creature.
> The covenant assures, "Never again."
>> Never again slaughter by God.
>> Never again holy violence.
>> Never again humanity in jeopardy.
>> Never again because such violence contradicts covenant.

The "never again" of blessing and covenant is given video performance:

A bow!
We call it "rainbow."
But it is bow as weapon,
> as in "bow and arrow,"
>> a killing instrument,
>> a lethal threat.

The bow, now hung in the sky by God's own self, is now retired from active duty:
> Never again, never, never again!

God's creation has been made safer, more secure.
This is a perfect narrative, promise from the Lord of the flood to the survivors of the flood.
The threat recedes as the waters have receded.
> *Except* that the narrator adds a note about this rescued family.

Noah engaged in self-indulgence, an indulgence that is not at all condemned.
> Except that he was made vulnerable and was exposed.
> The villain is predictably, Ham, the progenitor of Canaan.

Now the word "Canaan" is uttered in the text.
> This the first use of the term in the Bible. The utterance of this name evokes all of Israel's hostility and animosity.

"Canaan" is mentioned in order that his father may be indicted. There is no mention of him as "Black," as the later racist tradition.
The trouble is that Ham *peeked*.
> He looked as his father, Noah, lay drunk and naked.
>> He imposed on his father's privacy.
>>> He saw him naked.

> He violated the rule: You shall not uncover the nakedness of your father.

We are not told what he saw or what he thought.
> But it is enough.
>> It is enough to evoke a curse from Father Noah,
>>> a curse of enslavement and depravation,
>>>> setting up Shem and the Israelites for pre-eminence.

We get both in our memory:
> We get the exhibit of the rainbow of *fidelity*;
> we get the sordid account of human *depravity*.

It has been our destiny to juggle and adjudicate
> to treasure the rainbow of fidelity,
>> to recall later in the exile a like assurance (Isa. 54:9–10),
>> to manage wanton probes that threatened the dignity of the family,
>> as though "nakedness" is a cipher for exposure and humiliation.

We go on and on with that adjudication:
> It is like choosing life or death;
> It is like choosing prosperity or adversity;
> It is like choosing blessing or curse.

Noah died after 950 years, long enough!
> He left for us a mixed legacy,
>> leaving us hard work to do,

hard work made more so by our preoccupation with "Canaan"
> or some other abiding enmity.

We—all of us—are strange mixes of trust and self-indulgence.

We are glad to be on the receiving end of your magisterial promise;
but we also look away to our appetites and desires.
Claim us more fully for your peaceful order.
Weave us into the orbit of your generous rule. Amen.

ON READING GENESIS 10

> *"Can you lift up your voice to the clouds,*
> *so that a flood of waters may cover you? . . .*
> *Who can tilt the waterskins of the heavens,*
> *when the dust runs into a mass*
> *and the clods cling together?"*
> *(Job 38:34, 37–38)*

We are not alone. We never are.
   We are surrounded by a great cloud of witnesses.
      Sometimes they ground us into a solid identity.
      Sometimes they spook us with odd, eerie presence.
Either way, we travel in a company.
   In times of anxiety and in times of pride,
      we seek to locate ourselves more precisely.
   We devise genealogies that organize and chart and relate.
   Our good mothers and fathers mapped out a genealogy of faith,
      locating us among the three sons of Noah, the three brothers.
   In this scheme, all humanity derives from this triad,
      Japheth, Shem, and cursed Ham.
We can identify our allies, our rivals, our enemies,
   all make the list; no one is left out.
Japheth is quickly summarized. Not much interest to us,
   with their lands, their language, their families, their nations.
Ham gets a longer pause.
   His line yields Nimrod, mighty hunter,

> progenitor of great empires, Accad, Babel, Assyria,
>> all remembered as ferocious threats.

Shem, the well beloved, is our own father in faith.
What a family reunion that could be!
> What a convoluted, conflicted assembly!
>> No doubt why we never meet together.

The whole lot of the three is situated geologically:
> At the outset: "After the flood" (v. 1).
> At the conclusion: "After the flood" (v. 32).

We are beset at beginning and end by the flood.
The flood is attestation to the ultimate authority of YHWH, the flood maker.
The flood is a witness to our own penultimate status, answering to the Lord of the flood waters.
> The flood haunts us with our precariousness,
>> every time we hear news of flood, or hurricane, or cyclone—
>>> or for that matter sword, or famine, or pestilence.

We bow before you, master of the flood:
> our times are in your hands;
> our lives depend on your buoyancy;
> our futures line up to the edge of your churning waters.

We are three, we brothers, we brothers from Noah.
We are at risk, as the waters lap at the earth.
> But for now we prosper,
> son after son, after son, after son,
> and no less so, daughter after daughter.

It is all symmetrical and well-ordered, balanced and coherent.
> *Except* that along with the three of us,

Canaan, as a fourth, gets his own paragraph.
Canaan interrupts the symmetry.
Canaan sets our teeth on edge, the mighty "other,"
Canaanite might be a different bloodline, but not
   likely.
   More likely, Canaanite is a social class,
      the elite who looked down on us.
Canaan — issuing in seven nations,
   all a threat to us,
   all to be destroyed,
   all subject to *herem*:
The Hittites, the Girgashites, the Amorites, the Canaanites, the Perizites, the Hivites, the Jebusites.
We imagine them and name them and fear them.
In the midst of Canaan, we children of Shem get the land,
   "From Mesha to the hill country," land of promise!
We are glad, in your presence, to acknowledge our proper place of blessing.
   We are nevertheless left restless and precarious.
      We are at best penultimate.
We live, not from ourselves, but from your good gifts.
We receive your promises and walk in them.
We are indeed "after the flood,"
   mindful of your terrible power,
      aware of our vulnerability,
giving thanks for a safe place we do not readily share.

We do our best to understand and control the world in which we live.
We mobilize our best science along with our most mature faith.

But you, in your majesty, continue to outflank our best learning.
Give us the grace to live in good human community,
and the greater grace of our penultimate place in your creation. Amen.

ON READING GENESIS 11

For the LORD of hosts has a day against all that is proud and lofty,
against all that is lifted up and high . . .
against all the high mountains,
and against all the lofty hills;
against every high tower,
and against every fortified wall . . .
The haughtiness of people shall be humbled,
and the pride of everyone shall be brought low;
and the LORD alone will be exalted on that day.
(Isa. 2:12, 14–15, 17)

Now we get a story and another list. The list continues the genealogy of 10:21–31 concerning Shem. (We have no more interest in the futures of Japheth and Ham, now only our faith father Shem.) As our memory draws closer to the present tense of our narrative, matters become more precise. In the final entry here, we even get mention of women—no small matter amid a patriarchal index! We get Sarai, wife of Abraham, and Milcah, wife of Nahor. We hear no more of Milcah. The target of the entire list has been Sarai, wife of Abraham, daughter-in-law of Terah. Terah died. Now simply Sarai—and she is "barren"! The mighty line of Shem, moving to Abraham, now has a barren mother—end of line, no hope, no possibility, no future, no prospect. Our chapter ends with this breathtaking, hope-ending disclosure. No wonder the genealogy comes to an end. No more names on offer. The chapter leaves us waiting; the wait will be long. But it is a wait, not an end in despair, at least not yet.

The narrative of the tower interrupts the genealogy. But it would! The narrative of empire-building always disrupts the account of vulnerable families. The narrative of the tower appears abruptly, without introduction. We listen as the powerful flex their predatory muscles.

They propose to build—they always do
(right up to Trump Tower).

The Lord came down;
the Lord saw;
the Lord said;

> The tower-builders had imagined their autonomy; they always do!
>
> They had not anticipated such an awesome, insistent building inspector.
>
> They had clear plans.

But the Holy One brought confusion (*bll*) on them.
The Lord scattered them.

> Their ambitious plans ended in confusion and scattering.
>
> They could not prevail against the Lord of all languages who wills diversity.
>
> They could not prevail, even through their greedy ambition.

End of their story . . . for now.
And so the list from Shem can continue.
We always stand before you, holy God;

> We stand before you with our ambitious plans for building and for control.
>
> We stand before you as a member of a family roster.
>
> We want, much too often, grand architecture that will make old family lists passé.

And now, we are sobered yet again,

to discover that our plans for control cannot succeed,
to learn that we cannot gather the world into our proposed unity,
to recognize that our ambition is penultimate to your governance.
So yet again, we return to the old family roster.
We discover that our elemental belonging locates us.
We are glad, in the end, for that most durable roster, even when it includes our share of cowards, thugs, and embarrassments.
Our identity does not yield to our pride or our ambition.
So we meet you, as always, along with our family.
It is the good, blessed family of Shem.
Sometimes it is the family of all humankind, clear back to Noah.
Sometimes it is the family of all creatures, all the way back to Eve and her husband.
However constituted as family of Shem, or Noah, or Eve,
we come—all of us—to you,
faithful governor who will not be mocked or compromised, or detracted by our whims.
We end waiting, along with Mother Sarai,
glad for our wide kinship.

We have our family lines and our family memories and our family pedigrees. We cannot fail to recognize, amid these lines, memories, and pedigrees, that we have instances of moral failure, shameful conduct, and embarrassing kinfolk. We marvel that you continue to be a gracious God even for us with our several streaks of self-serving greed and fear. Amen.

ON READING GENESIS 12

By faith Abraham obeyed when he was called to set out for a place that he was to receive as an inheritance; and he set out, not knowing where he was going. . . . For he looked forward to the city that has foundations, whose architect and builder is God.

(Heb. 11:8, 10)

You were abrupt with our faith father, Abram.
You spoke only a terse imperative to him: "Go."
    That was all; except that you named his destination, requiring him to trust your guidance.
        It is a land yet to be disclosed, kept in the secret of your will.
Father Abram was to travel light, leaving all behind;
    He took with him only your blessing,
Only your blessing to be shared with the nations.
Your promise is singularly to Abram and his people;
    but the nations are in purview, always a part of his life with you.
The Lord of Abram is the God of the nations.
    Abram is never without the nations who would share the blessing.
Abram was as terse as you were; he was terse in like manner:
He went!
    He did not ask or wonder;
        He did not flinch or vacillate;
            He went, as we say, "by faith."
                He took nothing extra, except he traveled with a great company.
He reached the land; alas, it was a land of famine.

It was to be a land of blessing; but he found it in
a wave of hunger.
He went, as we always did in such need, to Egypt —
the place of ample food.
Our faith mother, Sarai, was beautiful. Did you
think it could be otherwise?

She was too beautiful for Abram's well-being.

Father Abram lied — because he was scared.
He willingly forfeited his wife, Sarai, for the sake
of his own safety.

In the end, his ruse did not work; but he was kept safe.
Abram is situated between a promise from God
and his own lie.
He did not think the promise would suffice;
He sought to supplement the promise by his
deception.
But his deception fooled no one.

Perhaps better if he could have trusted in your promise.
And now we, his heirs, live in his old ambiguity.

We are children of your promise.
We do not find it easy to trust the promise,
so we try to supplement it.
At the same time, we are children of his lie,
never sure enough about the promise.

*Mostly we are glad to settle where we are. Now and
then, however, we know ourselves to be summoned out
beyond our safe places. We are summoned to new tasks,
new obedience, and new risk. Mostly we are a mix of
obedience and reluctance. In the face of your summons
to us, we pray for courage to host your newness, and
for boldness in receiving your fresh summons. Amen.*

33 / ON READING GENESIS 12

ON READING GENESIS 13

> *Why are he and his offspring hurled out*
> *and cast away in a land that they do not know?*
> *O land, land, land,*
> *hear the word of the LORD!*
>
> (Jer. 22:28–29)

It was always about the land.
It was from the beginning, from the first utterance, about the land.
The impetus for our travel was your promise to us about the land,
    the one flowing with milk and honey.
We set out, Father Abram and Mother Sarai, all of us,
    toward the land.
When we arrived in the land of promise,
    it was not flowing with milk and honey.
    But it was a land full of herds and flocks,
        a land full of silver and gold,
            rich, fertile, ample, abundant!
The land was rich;
    but it could not support us all in one place.
    It would have been grazed to death.
    Land, as it always does, caused quarrels.
Generous Abram, our faith father, knew what to do to interrupt the quarrel.
    He offers his nephew, our cousin Lot,
        a choice of land.
        Abram was generous, surely because he trusted
            your promise.
Lot chose east, down from the Jordan.

His people — our cousins Moab and Ammon —
> settled there and continued there.

Our Father Abram, trusting in your promise, gladly took the land west of the river.

It was a peaceable settlement; it satisfied all parties. Our Father Abram had a moment of peaceable satisfaction grounded in his ready generosity.

He trusted the promise;
> he knew he had been blessed;
>> he savored the land; he loved the land;
>>> he gladly received the full promise of land from you.
>>> He knew it was a gift.

And so he worshipped;
> He uttered praise and thanks for your promise kept.

All that way he came, with his flocks and his herds,
> all the way to Hebron.

At Hebron, the city shrine,
> soon to be the tribal headquarters,
> soon to be a place of covenant-making in Israel,
> soon to be Abram's burial site,

at Hebron he worshipped the land-giving God,
> glad to place himself on the receiving end,
> grateful to the God of all real estate.

He walked the land, end to end,
> every step an exercise in gratitude,
>> awed by the unspeakable gift now entrusted to him.

The land is unfailingly such an attraction, and we want to possess it. The land is always such a seduction, and we are lured by it. We are glad that we live "in the land of the free and the home of the brave." But we are never free of our legacy of occupation, extraction, extermination, and genocide. Land attracts and it seduces. There is so much for which we must repent to you, Lord of all our lands. Amen.

ON READING GENESIS 14

Prepare war. . . .
Beat your plowshares into swords,
and your pruning hooks into spears;
let the weakling say, "I am a warrior."
(Joel 3:9, 10)

We may imagine the scene:
Father Abram and Mother Sarai listen to the news. The Palestinian Broadcasting System (PBS for short) reports a disturbing war swirling around the Dead Sea.
They listened with chagrin, appalled at the violence. But then they heard this:
    Their nephew Lot had been taken captive.
    Abram and his nephew had long since parted from each other in a most friendly way.
    But the uncle still cared for the nephew.
Now what had been interesting becomes a compelling summons.
    Abram acted quickly and decisively.
        He rescued Lot and his property,
            yet another act of fatherly compassion!
Upon that quick, decisive rescue,
    Abram worshipped.
He did not call you by your covenantal name, YHWH.
    He received a blessing through your earlier, more generic name, "God Most High."
        He knew the name; he knew the name signified your great lordly sovereignty.

He never doubted your presiding authority.
He worshipped you in thanks for the safe rescue.
He sang, along with his priest, doxologies to you.
He put his money where his doxological mouth was
. . . he tithed.
He refused the offer of booty.
We give thanks that we are in the train of Father Abram.
We are thankful for his piety,
> for his readiness to trust your good gifts,
> for his sense of having enough without taking more.

We are mindful that right in the midst of world conflict and jeopardized family,
> he trusted, he worshipped, he gave rather than took.

We can do no more than to sign on with his faith,
> refusing the greed of the world around us,
> content with the gifts you have given us.

We end, alongside Father Abram, with a deep, honest, simple "thank you."

Imagine! The superpowers posture and rattle weapons in each other's faces. We as the US superpower posture alongside the kings of Shinar, Ellasar, and Elam. It is as if the superpowers cannot help ourselves from such aggressive posturing. In the midst of such conduct, Father Abram worshipped and tithed. Give us the freedom of Father Abram to respond to your governance. Give us courage beyond Father Abram to be at the work of peacemaking; we do not doubt it is your work! Amen.

ON READING GENESIS 15

Those who wait for the LORD shall renew their strength,
they shall mount up with wings like eagles,
they shall run and not be weary,
they shall walk and not faint.

(Isa. 40:31)

Father Abram lived in a world with ready access to you, the God of promise.

He had easy conversation with you.

Abram himself is a bundle of anxiety (not unlike us),
    fretting because he had no son,

              no heir,

      no one to receive his great promise from you.

You spoke to him three times:

    You spoke to him, and promised him an heir from his own body.

        It was an audacious promise, made to an old man with an old wife.

        Your promise was an assurance that your promise would live.

    You spoke to him that his offspring, the one you promised, would be enslaved.

        You anticipated the enslavement by Pharaoh, king of Egypt.

        You knew about the long suffering to come on the people of Abram,

        but you promised deliverance . . . with great possessions!

        You the promise maker would be the great emancipator.

You spoke to Father Abram at twilight.
> You envisioned an expansive land of promise,
>> reaching all the way north and all the way south.

You spoke three times, each time a wondrous promise.
And then, it is reported,
> Father Abram trusted the promise;
>> he believed your good word.
>>> He relied on our faithfulness.

This is his "righteousness," his qualification before you.
> His life consisted in betting his future on your good promise.

So it is with us:
> you make promises to us;
> you make promises to us that contradict the world we see in front of us.
>> We have a chance to trust your good word,
>>> to embrace the world you resolve to give.

We are, like Father Abram, a mix of faith and expediency.
> But upon this fresh hearing of your good word,
>> we take fresh hope for your future,
>>> the assurance of things hoped for,
>>> the conviction of things not seen.

Your promise outruns our present tense. In our honesty, we know that we cannot receive your promise while we cling to our old selves and our old treasures. We pray for trusting faith that we may yield what we have in hand in order to receive your new gifts that await us. Give us gratitude that matches your generosity. Amen.

ON READING GENESIS 16

He gives the barren women a home,
making her the joyous mother of children.
(Ps. 113:9)

The drama of Father Abram and Mother Sarai is an early version of *The Handmaid's Tale*.
Everything for them hinged on your gift of an heir.
    But there was no heir given to them,
            no son was born to them,
            no future was kept open for them.
In her anxiety over her barrenness, Sarai
    acts boldly and decisively.
    She assigns Abram a slave-girl mistress.
        The matter is immediately complex for all parties.
    Sarai rejects her own initiative; she blames Abram.
    Abram abdicates responsibility.
    The slave-girl, Hagar ("the sojourner"), runs away in fear and desperation.
Looking back at our faith family,
    we see that this was a real crisis,
        with real emotions,
        with hard futures.
    Every character is vexed beyond bearing.
We might have wished for a family less complicated and compromised,
    but our faith family, like many families, is deeply complicated.
We might have wanted a simple conventional family with one mother, one father, and us.

But there she is in the midst of our faith family—
Hagar!
> To some in the family, she is an awkwardness, an embarrassment, a disruption.

Abram and Sarai must act out the drama of many families,
> coping with an inexplicable child who is quite "other,"
>
> one with real claims to be taken seriously.

For this instant, our reading turns to Hagar.
> She requires text time.
>> We watch as she plays out her role;
>>
>> she is desperate; she runs away, perhaps she will die.

But no! An angel from YHWH reaches her.
> She is not beyond the reach of the Holy One.
>
> She is not outside the purview of divine care and providence.
>
> The angel takes Hagar as a legitimate recipient of divine kindness.

Imagine! The power of God reaches out beyond "our mother and our father"
> to this third party, seen as an awkward embarrassment—but not by God.

Everything in Hagar's future turns on the angelic promise,
> a future-generating word.
>> She will have a son;
>>
>> he will be named Ishmael;
>>
>> she is seen by God;
>>
>> Ishmael will be an outlier in the world, never fully in.

So the family adapts. It reckons with reality, as it must.

It acknowledges the outcome of its circumstance.
The family photo now includes this "wild ass" of a man.
The family will now be marked for its future;
it will live with its awkwardness.
At hand is Mother Hagar—that is who she is now—
Mother Hagar is capable of piety.
She marveled that the Great God of promise had seen her;
she was not beyond the pale of divine horizon;
she is embraced in the care of God.
Abram and Sarai may have wished otherwise,
but they could not limit God's reach.
They could not curb the compassion of God for this "intruder."
Our narrative of faith family is complex and complicated.
But it matters not at all to you.
You are the God who sees and knows and blesses.
We are astonished that we live in your world,
seeing you override our limits,
interrupting our genealogies,
welcoming those whom we would exclude.
Hagar is a cipher for your awkward disturbances of our preferred familial arrangements,
for the ones excluded by Abram and Sarai, you are the God of welcome.
In our amazement we are grateful.

We know about barrenness when the future is closed and we can find no way forward. But we also know that you are the God who makes a way out of no way.

We trust your capacity to create for us new possibilities. Override our needy despair with your future-making power. We will wait for new possibilities that come only from your open hand. Amen.

ON READING GENESIS 17

Like arrows in the hand of a warrior are the sons of one's youth.
Happy is the man who has a quiver full of them.

(Ps. 127:4–5)

Our faith father, Abram, is at 99 years an old man.
    He is wedded to an old woman, Sarai.
In his old age, he is addressed by the Lord, God Almighty.
    He is invited into covenant;
        he is promised a multitude from his semen;
            he is given a new name, Abraham;
                he is pledged land.
His life belatedly comes to rich fulfillment,
    this after long years of disappointed waiting.
    He is marked by circumcision,
        a physical marking linking him to the God of all promises.
So also for old lady, Sarai.
    She gets a new name, Sarah, the princess!
    She receives a blessing of multitudes from her womb.
Abraham speaks only to question the Holy One who makes promises:
    Can a child be born . . . ?
    Can Sarah . . . ?
He is willing to settle for Ishmael, the only son she has.
Ishmael, that son, is blessed and given promises.
Abraham's future is circumscribed only by the divine "but."
    No, but your wife Sarah shall bear you a son.
    But my covenant I will establish with "Isaac."

The unborn son is named . . . end of conversation.
Abraham obeys the intrusive promissory voice:
> Ishmael is circumcised; for now, he is the heir.
> Ishmael receives a blessing.
> The divine "but" that anticipates Isaac qualifies and limits the future for Ishmael.

It strikes one that Abraham, in this long chapter,
> speaks only once.
> He speaks only to doubt;
> he never assents;
> he never responds to or answers the promise;
> he never actively receives it.

His silence, however, does not matter.
> The address from the Almighty is a unilateral utterance.
> It is a one-way conversation;
> it does not expect or wait for a response.

It is like that in the world where you preside.
> You are the mighty God who issues dictums,
> > who declares futures,
> > > who presides over our destiny.

We might wish for dialogue and interaction,
> but they are not required here.
> We are like aged Abraham and elderly Sarah,
> > and even the blessed Ishmael,
> > > living in a world of your powerful governance.

We are accustomed to making our way,
> to getting along,
> to coping when we lose,
> and to celebrating when we prevail.
> We are skilled in handling the unfolding of our lives.

But then you come with your lordly utterance.
   You outflank our best intentions.
   You override our self-sufficiency.
   You offer beyond all that we can think or imagine.
And we—what shall we do?
   We will receive you with praise.
   We will accept your surprises in gratitude.
   We will abide in awe of you,
      you who gives life to the dead;
      you who calls into existence things that do not exist.
We will, in amazement, live our lives on your terms,
   terms that may bless us when we are receptive,
   terms that may break us when we resist,
   terms that result in abundance beyond our own capacity.

"Everlasting" is a very long time, longer than all our years and all our hopes. You have made a promise to us for durable fidelity all for imaginable times to come. Give us the grace and the freedom to trust ourselves to your good promise. Let us act in the freedom of your fidelity that turns our lives back to you in glad, trusting obedience. Amen.

ON READING GENESIS 18

"For mortals it is impossible, but not for God;
for God all things are possible."
                              (Mark 10:27)

We catch Father Abraham in two roles,
   playing out two different dramas.
He is the generous host.
   His reception of his visitors leaves him a bit afraid.
   He has maybe three surprising guests, or maybe
      only one.
Either way, Abraham
   saw them,
   welcomed them,
   washed their feet,
   prepared a meal with Sarah and his servant, and
   stood by them as they ate.
But the visitors had not arrived in order to eat;
   they had come to make an announcement.
   They blurted it out:
      Sarah will have a son!
They knew her name, and they said her name out loud;
   It was something of a scandal.
The old couple had an odd, emancipated anticipation.
   The old lady laughed . . . (to herself);
   It was a stifled chuckle of embarrassment.
She knew that she, as well as the old man, was past sexual possibility.

The visitor (now one) chides her;
> then quizzes her:
>> Is YHWH limited?
>> Is YHWH incapable of miracle?
>> Is YHWH ruled by your definition of the possible?

The old couple do not answer; they have no answer, left speechless.

They know the right theological answer; but they also know their own condition
> that will not permit them to voice "the right answer."

The visitor hears her laugh of embarrassment. And then leaves.

And we are left to imagine;
> we will wait for "due season."
>> Then we will know if the "right answer" or their bodily reality will prevail.
> But we must wait, as they must wait.

Abraham is an advocate.
> He cares about Sodom because he cares for his nephew, Lot.
> Like God, Abraham knows about the big trouble in Sodom,
>> the land of aggressive insurrection against the creator.
> He thinks the disobedient city should be rescued for such a one as his own nephew.

As advocate, he makes his case against the danger YHWH poses to the city.

He bargains, he negotiates, he cajoles:
> What's your bottom line, God?

Is fifty righteous enough?
> Or forty-five, or thirty, or twenty,
>> or even ten?

Finally, in exasperation, he puts his deep question to God:
> Are you the judge?
> Do you do justice?
> Is it not just to save the righteous?

His reasoning does not work.
> The arithmetic is acceptable.
> God agrees to ten!
>> But Abraham cannot locate ten righteous.

We are left to see the outcome.

Father Abraham embodies faith before God:
> On the one hand, as generous host he is submissive to God;
> On the other hand, as advocate he will confront God.

Lively faith requires of us both roles.
> So we submit to you, Lord of our lives,
>> welcoming you in the most lavish ways we can.
> So we challenge you, judge of your world,
>> calling you to generous justice,
>> asking you to curb punishment,
>> showing yourself compassionate.

We refuse to be only submissive, because we have cases to plead.

We refuse to be only advocate, because we know you command us for your purposes.

As you seek for such suppleness from us,
> so we pray for freedom that we may play both our roles,
>> with energy, courage, and imagination.

We leave you with two questions you have yet to answer for us:
    Is anything too hard for you?
    Shall the judge not do justice?
If Father Abraham is your confidant as you say,
    we dare wait for clarification.
We do not crowd your holiness,
    but we live in hope of your honesty with us.

We dare to pray and to hope beyond our competence. We do so, even while we trim you down to our size, holding you within the confines of our imagination. And then . . . we are surprised that you break beyond our limited imagination to do what the world judges to be impossible. We soon arrive at the limit of our capacity. We look beyond ourselves and find you and your wondrous readiness to do what we ourselves cannot devise. Amen.

ON READING GENESIS 19

Remember Lot's wife. Those who try to make their life secure lose it, but those who lose their life will keep it.

(Luke 17:32–33)

It is so strange to ponder Sodom, such an evil city,
   to discover your good governance even there.
Who would have dispatched "messengers" to such a place?
Who knew that nephew Lot was a host of hospitality?
   Or that thugs in the city would assault the visitor?
   Or that the visitors would protect Lot?
Who knew that rescue and protection could happen even there at your behest?
Nephew Lot receives special attention.
   He has been cared for by Father Abraham.
   He has been protected by angels.
And now he is rescued by the angels, kept alive amid the destruction.
But oh, the devastation!
   You creator God, in your righteous indignation,
      worked mighty violence.
   You show yourself impatient with evil,
               intolerant of it
                      capable of massive retaliation.
You did the big "overthrow."
We had imagined you to be loving and kind and gentle,
   but here we see that evil has no permit to prevail
      in your world.

We see that along with love and kindness and gentleness,
> you are an uncompromising force unloosed for justice.

You do move in mysterious ways,
> ways beyond our expectation or calculation.
>
> You do align yourself with justice, and you call creation to account.

We take nephew Lot as a cipher for your patient attentiveness,
>> for your protective exceptions,
> for your fidelity to your people of special claim.

We dwell in astonishment,
> noticing your steadfastness,
>> witnessing your fierce anger.
>
> We cannot reduce you to a system or a formula or a syllogism,
>> because you are loose as an active agent in the world.

As you refuse every reduction of yourself to our size,
> so we imagine you invite us to probe your inscrutable ways,
>
> not to settle easily,
>> but to require honesty and humility.

You have bet so much on nephew Lot—
> as we have seen, he is compromised in his role as father,
>
> sire of our illegitimate cousins.

Out of the stir of
> your mercy-justice or
> your justice-mercy,

comes our more complicated family.

We are a collage of cousins who fit no easy genealogical chart,
    occupying the earth,
    bred into our history,
    lingering in our memory.
You have an itch to govern,
    and we are left in wonderment
        beyond our thin-faced expectations.
You defy our reasoning,
    and we yield in awe to you,
        beyond our best decipherment.

We are stunned by the extent and depth of your mercy. You hoped not only for Father Abraham who walked in your way. You cared as well for nephew Lot in his waywardness. Your attentiveness is not measured by or limited to our small horizons. We give thanks for the wide, long reach of your goodness. Amen.

ON READING GENESIS 20

By faith he received power of procreation, even though he was too old
—and Sarah herself was barren—
because he considered him faithful who had promised.
(Heb. 11:11)

We have been here before.
> We have watched Father Abraham in his fear.
> We have ached as Mother Sarah is made a pawn of his fear.
> We have observed our faith father lie to save his skin.
> We have seen an adversary of Father Abraham come to the rescue,
> save Sarah, and
> reward Abraham.

You loom large in this narrative, Lord God.
> You are the one who warned Abimelech.
> You are the one who intervened to save all parties.

Father Abraham . . . not so good.
> He asks his Sarah to lie, or
> as he says,
> "do this kindness" (*hesed*) (20:13);
> some "kindness," to engage in willful deception!

Only later (late indeed!), does Father Abraham come to his senses:
> He prays;
> he prays for Abimelech,
> and God heard.

You are writ large in this narrative of deception.
You are writ large in all our narratives.

You are writ large to overcome our fearful deception.
You are the escape from all our self-deception.

    The narrative pushes beyond the sexuality of Abimelech,

              beyond the fear of Abraham,
            beyond the vulnerability of Sarah;

finally we come to you, the ultimate subject of all our stories.

Father Abraham is a strange mix of faith and fear. He trusts God, yet he takes matters into his own clumsy hands. We are like him, a mix of faith and fear. We pray that your perfect love may cast out our fear, letting us rely solely on your good faithfulness. Amen.

ON READING GENESIS 21

*But the other woman corresponds to the Jerusalem above;
she is free, and she is our mother....
Now you, my friends, are children of the promise, like Isaac.*
(Gal. 4:26, 28)

Sarah had a baby! A boy! An heir!
   It is the long-awaited, long-promised son,
      the heir the narrative has required.
The son/heir is a gift from God to this old couple of the promise.
He is named "Laugh."
   Mother Sarah had laughed.
      It is the same laugh we will laugh at Easter,
         when God has yet again prevailed against all odds.
Mother Sarah laughed,
   in joy,
      maybe with a bit of awkward embarrassment,
         perhaps grasping the irony of a birth to a couple well beyond childbearing.
The laugh of Sarah and the life of "Laugh"
   echo through the entire narrative.
   God has a made a way out of no way.
   The old couple can rest easy with an assured future for their family.
Sarah finishes the paragraph with a "yet": "Yet I have borne him a son" (v. 7).
   She is a defiant contradiction of the facts on the ground.

> This is a son of miracle, and Sarah receives him
> as such.

We expected a more extended story of this wondrous son/heir.
> But instead,
>> we get Ishmael, the abiding embarrassment to
>> the old couple.
>> Sarah wanted the awkward son of Abraham
>> expelled.
>> Docile Abraham obeys her.
>> The boy (and his mother) are sent away.

But not before the boy receives a blessing from God.
> He now has only bread and a skin of water,
>> but he will be a great nation.

He will be a great nation that will forever vex the family of "Laugh."

The rejected son receives God's assurance.
> God said to the boy, "Do not fear."
> God went with the boy and his mother.
> God continues to value the boy received by the
> Holy Couple.
>> Ishmael will have a long career outside of
>> Israel,
>> but nonetheless a bearer of God's promise.

He embodies all of the fearful "other,"
> perhaps even to present-day Palestinians.

"Laugh" may have his way,
> but he will not remain unvexed by his sibling,
>> because "the other son" will be present,
>>> living just beyond chosenness.

The story of Father Abraham is, ever again, a tale of coming to terms with the "other."
> Ishmael is made to be the "other"

> and now in this narrative Abimelech is yet
> another "other."

Abraham will make peace and establish covenant. Before he finishes with Abimelech, he will invoke El Elyon,
> the high God here identified as YHWH, God of Israel.

Abraham knows the covenantal name of God.
> But with Abimelech, the "other,"
>> he appeals to the name of God known and shared beyond Israel.

The God of Israel has a long beneficial reach beyond Israel to the "other."
So now "Laugh," the wave of Israel's future with God, is set down
> amid the other, Ishmael and Abimelech.

The God who delivered "Laugh" to Israel
> is the God who lingers as well with the "other."

"Laugh" has the big promise;
> but that big promise is not the whole story.
> The whole story is the God with mighty governance, even "in the land of the Philistines."

By the end of the chapter,
> we can imagine the old blessed couple
> exulting in the new baby boy.

They smile, they laugh, they exult,
> likely they dance in celebration,
>> not yet needing to reckon with demanding perils still to come.

We finish in celebration with them,
> but mindful that your governance
> is not fully contained,
> not even in their precious son.

Isaac is an inexplicable gift from God. His birth causes Mother Sarah to laugh; her laugh is a loud Easter laugh. She knows that she has defied all conventional reality because of God's power for life and God's faithfulness to promise. Grant that we may, like her, laugh a laugh of wonder and gratitude, awed by your life-giving capacity. Amen.

ON READING GENESIS 22

> *"The LORD gave, and the LORD has taken away;
> blessed be the name of the LORD."*
>
> *(Job 1:21)*

The old couple celebrated the new baby named "Laugh."
  But not for long!
  Soon enough the God who miraculously gave them the son
    now takes a fresh initiative.
  God is not yet certain about Father Abraham,
    whether his trust is genuine and reliable.
  He tests Father Abraham:
    Take your well-beloved son!
      OFFER HIM!
Then son given is now the son at great risk.
Father Abraham does not flinch;
  he obeys: wood, donkey, son!
No wonder the son is bewildered.
  He sees the wood and the donkey, but no lamb for sacrifice.
  Had his father forgotten?
  He wonders.
The father, yet again unflinching, answers with confidence.
  We do not know what he thought,
              or what he felt.
We know what he said:
    The Lord will provide.
    The verb is *ra'ah*, everywhere else taken as "see."

The Lord will see (= video);

The Lord will see beforehand (= pro-video).

We wonder: Did Abraham tremble as he reassured his son?

Did he think twice?

Did he want to turn back and scuttle his effort?

We are not told;

but we are told this:

He took the knife to kill his son, his only son.

He is poised to kill the son for whom he had waited long years, all his life.

He found the command of God to override his love for his son.

At that daring, awesome moment,

God called to Father Abraham as he had called him at the beginning of the chapter.

God called; he repeated the name of the father: "Abraham, Abraham."

There is urgency in the voice of God,

urgency to deter the father from his ready obedience,

urgency to save the son who would keep the promise alive.

God called with urgency,

because the test was over.

God had not been sure about Father Abraham.

Now God is sure: "Now I know."

Better if God had been omniscient and had not required the test;

but God did not know,

and so required the test.

Now for the first time, Abraham looks away from the task he was about to perform.

He looks and sees a ram, a proper animal for sacrifice.
He completed the sacrifice as he stood alongside his beloved son.
He knew the name of the place, or he devised the name:

God will provide.
God will see ahead of time.
God will pro-video;
God will be pro-vidential;
all is well for the father and for his son.

And so God will reiterate the great promise yet again.

The son will live; the promise will persist.
The father is vindicated in his trust.

But the narrative leaves us to wonder:

What father would offer up his son like this?
What father indeed??
What father or mother would send a son or daughter off to mindless imperial wars as cannon fodder?
What father or mother would consign a son or daughter to drown in a surfeit of consumer goods?
What mother or father would risk a daughter or son by substituting technology for protective affection?

The answer, of course, is that we, many fathers and mothers,

are swept into ideology that makes us crazy,
not deep enough in our faith.

We flinch before the command.
We compromise to get along.

And so Abraham stands before us as a mighty summons.

We give you thanks for your summons to faith,
>> for your command to obey,
>> for your invitation to trust you.
Grant that we may trust your promise,
that we "look up" like Father Abraham looked up,
> and embrace a better way,
>> the way of trust that lets our futures be in your generous hands.

Abraham could not believe his ears when he heard God's command. He is, nonetheless, prepared to obey. Here he engages in no duplicity or manipulation as he does elsewhere. We are left to ponder how demanding this God might be toward us in a bid for our obedience. We may be drawing close to such a time of testing. We may pray for guidance, courage, and stamina for the facing of our hour. Amen.

ON READING GENESIS 23

If we live, we live to the Lord, and if we die, we die to the Lord;
so then, whether we live or whether we die,
we are the Lord's.

(Rom. 14:8)

Mother Sarah lived long
   and bore a son.
      She died in old age and required a burial.
This odd narrative features nothing more and nothing less than the purchase of a burial plot.
But what a purchase!
The Hittites — of all people — are Abraham's bargaining partners.
Abraham asks to be given a burial plot.
The Hittites agree to give him a plot.
Abraham specifies the place he wants, and offers to pay full price.
Ephron the Hittite wants to give the plot to Abraham.
Abraham insists on paying.
Ephron, in the guise of a disclaimer, names his price for the plot — 400 shekels.
Abraham agrees and pays.
It is a long process.
   Both parties understood the game.
      Abraham from the outset expected to pay; the Hittite expected to be paid.
They settled. Deal done!
Mother Sarah is buried with due propriety,
   not far from Hebron,
      the locus of Abraham's sojourn.

The report ends with a double "possession":

"... passed to Abraham as a *possession* ..."

"... passed from the Hittites into Abraham's *possession.*"

The process is duly witnessed and completed in proper legal fashion.

In part, this narrative honors Mother Sarah.

But in part, this narrative exhibits Abraham's legal possession of the land.

Abraham and all his family were sojourners,
 living off the land,
 grazing the land,
  but never owning the land.

And now the land is a "possession."

It is like the fulfillment of Abraham's most ancient promise.

It is like an anticipation of the later conquest of Joshua.

This is the God who makes promises and keeps them.

This is the family who trusts and receives the promise.

This is the tiny defining wedge of ownership
 that anticipates the endless conflict in the land of promise.

It is not a gift; it is a purchase.

Abraham has the title.

He is entitled!

This is the beginning of a long contestation not yet resolved.

We face the reality that your good gift is an occasion for conflict in which we, even our government,
 manage to stay embroiled.

While we may be grateful for your promise kept,
we may at the same time beg your forgiveness for
our inability to share that good gift.

Mother Sarah did the daily quotidian work of parenthood; she cooked and washed, nurtured and admonished. She did the daily work that kept the promise alive into the next generation. We may take her as a stand-in for all the unnoticed parents who do such future-creating work. We remember her—and them—with abiding gratitude. Amen.

ON READING GENESIS 24

There shall once more be heard the voice of mirth and the voice of
  gladness,
the voice of the bridegroom and the voice of the bride,
the voices of those who sing,
as they bring thank offerings to the house of the LORD.
                                                            (Jer. 33:10–11)

Until now all we have known of Isaac
  is that he is the long-awaited heir,
  born to the promise;
  but now he is an adult of marriageable age.
This long narrative, the longest in the book of Genesis,
  lines out an effective strategy
  that culminates in the marriage of Isaac.
At the outset, Abraham instructs his servant:
  He gives specific instruction concerning a wife
    for Isaac;
    she must be of his kindred;
    she must be willing to come be with Isaac;
    she must sign on for her role as a mother for
      the promise.
The servant, faithful to Abraham, follows his instructions in this serious business.
The scene is pervaded by covenantal loyalty (*hesed*): the servant prays for God's *hesed* toward Abraham; the servant prays that finding a bride for the son is a sign of God's *hesed* toward the father;
the servant affirms Rebekah as a signature of God's *hesed* to Abraham; in his third usage the servant adds to his formulaic speech, "faithful" (*'emeth*).

The servant meets Rebekah, daughter of Bethuel, at the well.

   She qualifies!

   She is fair and a virgin.

      The servant lavishes Rebekah with jewelry, surely an effective persuader!

Enter Laban, brother of Rebekah.

   Her brother sees the jewelry now worn by his sister;

      in response to seeing the jewelry,

         he welcomes the servant with eager hospitality.

The servant reiterates the plot for Laban.

   Upon his extended recital,

      the servant makes his bid to the brother;

         deal loyally (*hesed*);

         deal truly (*'emeth*).

Father Bethuel and brother Laban quickly assent: "Take her and go."

They did not quibble or demur, but promptly agreed.

   Perhaps they agreed because they found the entire process well laden with piety and much *hesed*.

Or perhaps they are moved by the jewelry.

   Wealth is richly on exhibit;

   wealth performs wonders.

      It matters; it matters to these hard-bargaining males.

After all, their daughter/sister is a great prize.

   She does not need to go cheaply.

The narrator may be teasing us.

   He may be shrewd in his mix of piety and jewelry.

The strategy is effective. The deal is consummated.

   It is indeed a covenant deal,

      but it is made by men who could add and calculate.

All parties participate in the game of bargaining and hospitality.
The servant took Rebekah on her camel
> along with her entourage of maids, an impressive performance of love assisted by wealth.
>
> Only belatedly Isaac himself enters the narrative.
>> Matters evolve rapidly.
>>
>> He saw the camels.
>>
>> Rebekah saw him.
>>
>> She presented herself.
>>
>> He took her and loved her.

This is an ordinary drama of an arranged marriage with both bloodlines and wealth protected.
But it is more than that.
> It is a performance of *hesed* by all parties.
>
> It is a performance of *hesed* by the God of promise.
>
> It is an assurance that the future of the promise is kept for yet another generation.

The narrator is not direct;
> much is tacit and implied.
>
> All things work together for good among these faithful covenant keepers.

We are yet again dazzled by you, God of all promises,
> by your underground governance,
>
> by your faithfulness to the next generation,
>
> by your gift of a future to this people of chosenness.

We are reminded by your hidden governance
> that the world is at your behest;
>
> you hold the world in your safe hands;
>
> you watch over your beloved.

You are the worker of the extraordinary
> "in, with, and under" the ordinary workings of humanity.

We are grateful to have small steps assigned to us in your concealed choreography that we call "history."

Getting our kids married to the right partners is an abiding preoccupation of parents. In our tale, Isaac was led providentially by the goodness of God to his wife. That providential outcome, moreover, was accompanied by great wealth. We may be grateful for such providential outcomes, even if we notice them only belatedly. When we notice, we may be like the servant of Abraham, giving thanks to you for the goodness of your providential care. Amen.

ON READING GENESIS 25

"Teacher, tell my brother to divide the family inheritance with me."
(Luke 12:13)

Father Abraham, by the promise of God, is the father of many nations.
- We have an inventory of that claim at the outset of this chapter.
- These "others" receive gifts from Abraham.
  - But Isaac, the real son,
  - receives "all from him."
- (We have an echo of this "all" with the Prodigal Son and his brother.
  - "All that is mine is yours.")
- The "others" are sent away.
  - The terrain is cleared for the one family that matters to the narrator.

Abraham finished his work,
- giving life to his beloved Isaac.
- He dies; he is buried with Mother Sarah,
  - on the plot of land he now "possesses."

The narrator pauses to trace out the reality of the "others,"
- bequeathed by Hagar via Ishmael.
- These "others" receive mention, but the single-minded narrator has no real interest in them.

Our attention returns to the family of blessing,
- now to the next generation.
  - Like Mother Sarah, this "fair virgin," Rebekah, is barren.

But prayer promptly changes that, permitting her pregnancy.

It was a disturbed pregnancy,
> leading Mother Rebekah close to despair.

But then she learned why her pregnancy was so disturbed:

the two yet to be born struggled in her womb,
> two peoples in contention,
>> two sons with profound upheaval for generations to come.

It was just as YHWH had assured her:
the older, ruddy and hairy . . . Esau;
the younger, grasping and gripping . . . Jacob.
> One a hunter, the other a quiet man.

We can see the trouble to come
> as the parents choose a preference for a favor.

The father drawn to the elder;
the mother loved the younger.
A sure recipe for conflict!

Now, immediately, the brothers are adults;
> Esau, back from the hunt, is a good guy, but a little slow;
> Jacob strikes one as quick and calculating,
>> ready for advantage.

The older is hungry; the quiet one has bread and soup, what better!?

> The ruddy one has not learned about delayed satisfaction;
>> he lacks discipline and easily yields to his appetite;
>>> he is bent on the present moment;
>>> his brother is quick to exploit.

Things happen quickly.

> Then outcome is a conflict that will govern the future.
> We watch the two brothers perform their inescapable roles.
>> It is like Cain and Abel all over again.
>> It is like Ammon and Absalom soon to come.
>> It is like the son of indulgence and his older, disciplined brother,
>>> the indulgent one "squandering his property in dissolute living"!
>
> All we have to go on is your divine oracle that anticipates the conflict
>> and the fateful inverted order of things.
>
> The brothers know nothing of the divine oracle.
> They know only their needs and wants.
>> Esau's appetite caused his forfeiture,
>>> a lesson suffered by every parent who seeks to instill self-discipline.
>> Jacob knows a bargain when he sees one,
>>> a birthright that cost him only a bowl of lentils.
>> He is chosen; he will advance his chosenness by his cleverness.
>
> The narrator is reticent.
>> He does not tell us more.
>> But we are clearly on notice:
>>> chosen brothers are unlike other brothers;
>>>> Some will prevail.
>>>> Some will self-destruct.
>
> The conflict belongs to this family;
>> it belongs to every family.
>
> We will watch the conflict play out;
>> we will hunch that through it all you are at work for your purpose.

The brothers are unable to outflank the promise,
a cause of deep disturbance between them.
We will hope and assume that their struggle serves
your purpose.

Sisters and brothers by design are to be in mutual support and affection. Much too often, they are at odds with each other because of money, property, or inheritance. We pray to you today, convener of families, on behalf of such sisters and brothers who struggle with each other in toxic, destructive ways. We ask that you move such siblings past covetous greed to engage in supportive relationships. Break the vicious cycles of hostility as only you can do. Amen.

ON READING GENESIS 26

"There was a man who had two sons. . . . Now his elder son was in the field;
and when he came and approached the house, he heard music and dancing."

(Luke 15:11, 25)

Like father, like son!
Like Father Abraham, son Isaac lies to save his skin.
   He does not mind putting his wife, Rebekah, at risk.
   His father's trust in God stretched only so far,
     and then he tried for self-sufficiency, alas!
Like father, like son, Isaac received the blessing.
   He is the heir; God, the gift-giver, withheld nothing from him.
Like father, like son, Isaac must deal with Abimelech, an embodiment of the "other" in the narrative.
   As always in that arid land, it was a dispute about water.
   Isaac, like his father, promptly moved on to elsewhere,
     assured of abundance wherever he went.
   He goes on to another place, another place of his inexplicable well-being.
   He finds water as he knew he would.
   The God of ample water settles him for a life of well-being.
     He names his new place *Rehoboth*,
         signifying an ample place of abundance.
         It will not be otherwise for him.

> He named a place *Shibah/Beer-sheba*,
>> a locus of much water and much ancestral preoccupation.

It may be that we are watching old stories being recycled for this new character.
> More likely, perhaps,
>> sons reiterate the lives of their fathers.
> They reiterate unwittingly,
>> possessing the same gifts,
>>> yielding to the same seductions,
>>>> practicing the same habits,
>>>>> counting on the same blessings.

We gladly affirm, God of all promises,
> that you have brought well-being to our faith ancestors.
> You have been there for them,
>> the giver of abundance,
>> the guarantor of their lives,
>> the generous guardian of their futures.

We are grateful for this legacy.
Give us the stamina to embrace the promise,
>> to rely on your fidelity,

to resist the temptation to self-sufficiency.
We gladly belong to this faith family that lives by your good gifts.

As we finish with this chapter on Isaac,
> we notice that Isaac gets thirty-three verses,
> Esau gets two verses.
>> He is an outlier to this family of promise;
>> he marries "outside,"
>>> away from his family of promise.
>> The couple of the promise ends the chapter "bitter."

All your generosity, and they feel slighted!
Give us perspective enough to see the ways your goodness outruns their vexation (and our vexation). We may be grateful for our fathers given us by God; We may be equally grateful for God-given freedom to depart from them.

> Either way, we may be grateful that our Heavenly Father overrides all our human arrangements through unmeasured generosity and fidelity.

We give thanks for fathers and mothers who bless their children. We pray for parents and for children who are estranged, and for sisters and brothers who dispute their inheritance. We thank you for good settlements grounded in your generosity and forgiveness. Amen.

ON READING GENESIS 27

Those who do not love a brother or sister whom they have seen, cannot love God whom they have not seen.

(1 John 4:20)

The well-beloved heir, Isaac
  has now become a father,
  old with failing eye sight.
    His dim vision is essential to the narrative:
      he is unable to distinguish between his two sons.
He is hungry; he wants a good meal before he dies.
    He summons his son, the son who is a hunter.
    He would, of course, summon his older son!
The plot thickens:
    Rebekah sees a chance to advance her favorite,
      the younger son who is no hunter.
    Rebekah knows that families are capable of such behavior,
      full of plots, intrigue, and calculations to seize advantage,
        gamesmanship that has no honor.
        The more the family possesses, the more of cunning manipulation.
Her son, her favorite, the one who does not hunt,
obeys her in deception.
    She fixes for the old man a meal of his favorites,
      she, not the son!
The son performs the deception.
    His voice nearly betrays him to his innocent, aged father.
    But not quite.

> > His ersatz hairy skin overrides his betraying voice.
> >
> > The father falls for his deception.
>
> The old man performs his fatherly function: He blesses.
>
> > It is as though the blessing, along with the meal, becomes his farewell before his death.
>
> The blessing he utters upon his seductive, thieving son is lavish:
>
> > dew in an arid land;
> >
> > grain and olive oil, the money crops of the land,
> >
> > preeminence among the nations with many subservient peoples,
> >
> > dominant in the family
> >
> > > with a capacity to bless or to curse.
>
> Jacob, in his deception, has received a blank check of well-being
>
> > from his beguiled father.
>
> It does not matter at all to the narrator that it is all a hoax.
>
> > A hoax is good enough
> >
> > > because the utterance of the old father is performative.
> >
> > What he says, he does.
> >
> > What he utters, he brings to reality.
> >
> > The father's word is in good faith with full effectiveness.
>
> It is all awry; it is all deception. It is all manipulation.
>
> > Too strong and too late to be recalled!
>
> So now Esau:
>
> > He comes to his father with his fresh hunt and with great expectation.
> >
> > He asks a blessing.

It is a pivotal moment in the life of the family, and in our narrative.

In a twinkling, the old man sees his mistake.

He knows it is a mistake beyond recall.

He knows that he has skewed and harmed the future of his family.

No wonder he "trembled violently,"

helpless in his disability.

Esau understood immediately what has happened.

The "violent trembling" of his father is promptly matched

by his pathos-filled cry.

The father and the son are trapped together in an instant of immense loss.

They sense together how their history and their future have gone askew.

The older son immediately sees his immense loss.

It is no wonder that he wept!

Who would not weep at such a robbery?

The grieving father manages a blessing for his older son.

The older son will live in hard places.

He will serve his brother, and then he will break free.

The younger son, the thief, must flee for his life before the banger of his betrayed brother.

His mother sends him away to safety.

For now, the narrative has no more interest in Esau.

The plot follows Jacob.

He must marry well to please his mother.

The drama of conniving mother, colluding son, trembling father, weeping brother altogether

is enough to take our breath away.

This family is *like every other family,* fraught with turmoil.
This family is *unlike any other family,* grounded in providential care.
This family invites from us recognition of our common lot.
It also causes us to marvel at its singular vocation.
We are left to turn to you, provider for all our families,
> that we may live well with loss,
> that we may trust your working of our future,
> that we may boldly voice our hurts in hope of your hearing.
> that we may find, amid our clever stratagems, the working of your good promises.

We are mindful of the many venues where siblings engage in hostility—Israelis and Palestinians, Hindus and Muslims, Catholics and Protestants. We give you thanks for the brave, people who engage in ministries of reconciliation. You are the giver of shared well-being; we ask for those gifts among us now. Amen.

ON READING GENESIS 28

The LORD was not in the wind;
and after the wind an earthquake, but the LORD was not in the earthquake;
and after the earthquake a fire, but the LORD was not in the fire;
and after the fire a sound of sheer silence.

(1 Kgs. 19:11–12)

Jacob must flee for his life.
    Before he departs as a fugitive,
        his father blesses him
        concerning land and multiple progeny.
    His father commends him.
    His father holds no grudge:
        he does not mention Esau;
        he does not recall the trickery;
        he is on program for the promise given to Jacob.
Then a quick promise to Esau as well:
    Esau knew about the mandate of his father to his brother:
        No Canaanite wife!
    Esau took his father's will seriously;
    he still hoped for a measure of well-being from his father;
    he took his wife from his cousin Ishmael.
But enough about Esau!
Jacob is enroute to Haran, the old family base.
    But he must sleep amid his dangerous escape.
        He sleeps; but it is a disturbed sleep.
    The dream he dreams is engagement with God's

>holiness amid his disturbed sleep.
>Jacob thought he was alone as he slept.
>He was desolate and abandoned.
>He anticipated at best a nightmare in his sleep.
>He did not know that the Holy One could occupy empty space of the wilderness.

It turned out that nothing depended upon what Jacob thought or what he knew.
Everything depended on the will of the Holy One.
Everything depended upon the disruptive speech of the Holy One.
> The one who speaks to Jacob is the God already known in Genesis,
>> the one who had addressed his grandfather and his father.

This holy utterance abounds in promise!
> This is the God who makes promises:

the land,
many offspring,
a blessing beyond Jacob to many other families.
>> (The "other" keeps showing up in Israel's narrative!)

But then the promise surges beyond a stylized recitation.
Now the promise is intimate and personal:
> I am with you;
> I will keep you;
> I will bring you back;
> I will not leave you;
>> 'Til I have done the promise in full.

This visitation—ladder and all—left Jacob stunned and in awe.
He marked the place:

House of God!
Gate of heaven!
No wonder he was fearful;
> he was in a place occupied by God's fierce holiness.

The Bible is like that!
> The God of the Bible is like that!
>> Places of desolation may become places of hope;
>> places of abandonment may become venues for accompaniment;
>> places of isolation may become places of visitation.

Jacob must respond to the Holy One.
> He responds,
>> but only as the trickster that he always is.
> His response is loaded with conditionality:
> IF!
>> If God will be with me;
>> if God will keep me;
>> if God will give me bread to eat;
>> if God will give me clothing to wear.

He wants a foolproof security system!
Then . . . only then:
> then you will be my God;
> then this will be God's house . . . Bethel;
> then I will tithe.

Jacob's response is perfectly symmetrical:
> three conditions/three commitments.

No commitments until his conditions are met.
> He bargains all the way to the bottom of his experience.

See we also:
> when we can turn this relationship into a transaction;
> when we seek to resolve covenantal trust into contractual correctness.

We may pray to be freed from such manipulation as Jacob is not,
> to live from trust and obedience
>> that counts fully on the Holy One.

We, like Jacob, live by promises.
> We pledge not to turn God's promises into negotiations;
> We resolve to be as self-giving as God in God's own self-giving is to us.

You surprise us by your presence. You meet us in our fearful nightmares. You confront us in the daylight of economics. You abide with us through our deepest loves. You come and go as you choose. We yearn for you and we tremble before you, because you are the great essential mystery of our lives. Amen.

ON READING GENESIS 29

"Look toward heaven and count the stars, if you are able to count them....
So shall your descendants be."

(Gen. 15:5)

The flight of the fugitive, running for his life,
   comes to its destination.
Jacob arrives at a well of living water.
   He connects with some shepherds from Haran.
Enter Rachel!
   But Jacob remains fixed on the sheep,
      and their need for water.
Finally . . . he sees Rachel!
   She is well-connected to the family.
   For a moment he disregards Rachel, still preoccupied with the sheep and their water.
Finally the narrative has Jacob see Rachel.
   He kissed her, as forward as he could be.
   He wept aloud.
   He sketched out family connections to Rachel.
Uncle Laban welcomes the fugitive who is a kinsman.
   He ran to him;
   he embraced him;
   he kissed him;
   he brought him into his house;
   he is stunned to find his kinsman, a fugitive no less.
Laban opens negotiations for wages,
   for Jacob will stay to work for Laban.
The narrative pauses in the bargaining to supply

essential information:
> two daughters:

Leah: older, lovely;
Rachel: younger, graceful, and beautiful.
Sharpie Laban agrees to the bargain:
- seven years for Rachel;
- seven quick years;
- seven years of deferred love.
  > All agree;
  > all celebrate;
  > all anticipate.

Except for Laban; he is a trickster in a family of tricksters.
- He upholds the custom of primogeniture;
- all is according to birth order,
  > the very custom Jacob himself had violated with his own brother.
- Jacob gives the custom of primogeniture no credence.
  > But here he has no choice:
  >> seven quick years!
  > Time flies when you are in love.

Finally he marries Rachel.
- He loves her!

Enter YHWH who has been monitoring the drama.
- In this instance, YHWH is on the side of primogeniture.
- YHWH blesses Leah ... an open womb!
- YHWH withholds the blessing from Rachel;
  - she is barren;
  - she is barren like old Mother Sarah;
  - she is barren like Rebekah before her;
  - mothers of the promise are uniformly barren!

Leah's open womb is fruitful and productive:
   a son Reuben . . . affliction;
   a son Simeon . . . because I am hated;
   a son Levi . . . joined to the Lord;
   a son Judah . . . praise the Lord.
Four sons — quickly — a rich abundance,
                       a blessing.
Rachel is held in thrall by the habit of primogeniture.
   She must wait on her older sister;
      the one less loved,
      the one more fruitful,
      the bearer of God's abundance: It must have rankled!
The chapter is about waiting.
   Rachel must wait for a child;
   Jacob must wait for Rachel.
   Neither Rachel nor Jacob protest or complain.
They accept God's gifts given in God's time.
   The narrator anticipates the Psalms:
      "Wait for the LORD;
         be strong; and let your heart take courage;
         wait for the LORD!" (Ps 27:14)
      "I waited patiently for the LORD;
         he inclined to me and heard my cry." (Ps. 40:1)
The affirmation of the psalmist is this:
   "He put a new song in my mouth,
      a song of praise to our God." (v. 3)
The Psalms are echoed by the prophet:
   "Those who wait for the LORD shall renew their strength,
      they shall mount up with wings like eagles,
   they shall run and not be weary,
      they shall walk and not faint." (Isa. 40:31)

We may imagine that Jacob did indeed renew his strength,
> to soar, run, and walk.

Such a wait is contrary to the "now" immediacy of our technological environment.
We easily imagine that with our technique we may have life as we want it when we want it.
> Speed is the order of the day.

But faith is otherwise: faith accepts God's slow time.
> In that slow time, gifts are given,
>> babies are born,
>> promises are kept.

It happens when we ease off the rush of our initiative.
Such a wait could not have been easy for Mother Rachel as she watched sister Leah prosper.
Such waiting could not have been easy for Father Jacob as he waited for fourteen years.
But they knew their times were in God's hands.
> So say we all in our sober acknowledgment
>> of being on the receiving end of good gifts from God.

You are the Lord of all life and from you come all our blessings. You will that we should have an abundant life. Give to us, as you gave to our ancient family, the capacity for life abundant. Let it be an abundance that thrives on generosity, kindness, and neighborliness. Amen.

ON READING GENESIS 30

"Whoever does the will of God is my brother and sister and mother."
(Mark 3:35)

At the outset, this chapter features the birth of many sons to Jacob.
 This has been a contest between his wives, the two sisters.
At the outset, Rachel reiterates the strategy of old Mother Sarah,
 a substitute wife here named Bilhah.
  Bilhah births two sons:
  Dan and Naphtali.
Leah competes.
 Her substitute, Zilpah, yields two sons:
 Gad and Asher.
Leah bears two more sons:
 Issachar and Zebulun.
 (And oh, yes, a daughter, Dinah;
 more on her later.)
When we add the initial four to Leah from the previous chapter
 (Reuben, Simeon, Levi, Judah),
 we get her number at a complete ten.
Leah is much blessed; Mother Rachel cannot compete;
 she has only the substitute.
We arrive at mid-chapter with the contest completed.
 Rachel still awaits a son!
 BTW, mandrakes are a plant taken to boost fertility.
 Clearly the fertility of the family of Jacob has been boosted,

whether by the magic of mandrakes
or by the mercy of God.
At the conclusion of the chapter,
Jacob the sharp bargainer and
his sharp bargaining father-in-law, Laban,
duel about wages, pay, and labor.
Jacob is dominating, a hard bargainer.
He asks only a little from his father-in-law,
only speckled and spotted sheep,
black lambs, and
spotted and speckled goats.
That is all!
He wants only the rare exceptions from the flocks
and herds.
Voilà! Jacob gets a lot of valuable animals.
The odds have been reversed.
The exceptions are everywhere on offer.
Jacob works his magic,
more animals, striped, speckled, spotted.
We are not told; but Laban must have been bewildered and begrudging.
Jacob gets all he needed or wanted.
The chapter ends in a summation of the blessed wealth of Jacob:
flocks,
enslaved men and women,
camels,
and donkeys.
Who could ask for anything more?
The presence of enslaved men and women in the narrative is jarring.
But they seem to come with great wealth.
Perhaps their mention is a harbinger of the way

in which son Joseph will reduce hapless Egyptian peasants to slavery (Gen. 47:21).

Thus:
> At the outset, many sons in an uneven competition,
> at the conclusion, the cunning Jacob made wealthy.

Between the competition and the report of wealth,
> in the center of our chapter,
> we get only two verses upon which everything depends.

Rachel—the barren one,
> a loser to her sister!
> God remembered Rachel!
>> God had long forgotten Rachel and left her barren.
>
> Now she is fertile.
>
> When God remembers,
>> good things happen.

Thus:
> God remembered Noah, and the flood waters subsided (Gen. 8:1).
>
> God remembered Abraham, and Lot was rescued (Gen. 19:29).
>
> God remembered Abraham, Isaac, and Jacob, and the exodus was put in motion (Exod. 2:24).

It is no wonder that the lamenting psalmist prays that God would not forget:
> The psalmist prays in dire straits:
>> "How long, O LORD? Will you forget me forever?
>>> How long will you hide your face from me?"
>> (Ps. 13:1)

The psalmist boldly asks in petition:

> "Do not deliver the soul of your dove to the wild animals;
> do not forget the life of your poor forever."
> (Ps. 74:19)

So, now, God remembers Rachel;
> she has been long forgotten;
> she has been long barren and bereft.
>> Now she is remembered!
>>> God overcame her barrenness;
>>> She bore a son!
>>> She bore a son who would carry the promise.
>>> She bore a son to continue the line of blessing.
>>> She bore a son, and the future is open.

We have to do with the God who opens futures,
> who makes for Rachel (and us) a way out of no way.

The mother names her son "Added."
> He is added to the sons of Jacob.
> He is added to the line of promise bearers.
> He is added to the roster of continuers.

Placed just between the competition that Rachel loses
> and the bargaining in which Jacob prevails,
>> just between,

we get a wonderment.
> Her reproach is ended.
> Her barrenness is overcome.
> Her shame and failure are vetoed.

She has prevailed . . . by the goodness of God.
> This moment in the center of the chapter attests what the Bible knows best.
>> We may be open to the surprises and gifts of God.
>>> She must have prayed; then God heard.
>> That is why we pray.

We pray in hope.
We pray in hope in hopeless circumstances.
We pray because we do not doubt the capacity of
> God to create futures.
>> This is the God who calls worlds into being.
>> This is the God who raises the dead.

So now God has added!
> Her life is not a zero-sum game.
> Nor is ours!

We are left astonished . . .
> and grateful.

We thank you that you have set the solitary in families. We thank you for the good blessing of sisters and brothers and siblings. Give us largeness of reach that we may recognize our many kinfolk beyond our local clan; grant that we may learn to live well, peaceably, and generously in your great family of humankind. Amen.

ON READING GENESIS 31

"The LORD is witness against you, and his anointed is witness this day, that you have not found anything in my hand."
And they said, "He is witness."

(1 Sam. 12:5)

Interaction between the father-in-law and the son-in-law is not easy.
> Both of them are aggressive, acquisitive, and bold.
> Both of them are demanding and calculating.
> The chapter details the way in which the two of them —
>> father-in-law and son-in-law —
> find a way to live peaceably with each other —
>> apart from each other.

The chapter readily divides into discreet dramatic episodes.

Jacob must depart.
> He is on the road again.
> His two wives, daughters of Laban, urge him to leave.
> The real impetus for his departure, however, is the summons of God:
>> The Lord said, "Return."
>> "The God of my father has been with me."
>> "God has taken away the livestock of your father."
>> God said, "Look up"!
>> This is the God of Bethel who said, "Leave, return."
>> His daughters said: Do what God says.

The chapter articulates compelling harmony between practical interest and divine guidance.
    Jacob must leave.
    He leaves with great wealth,
        a contrast with the poverty he had at the outset.
    He leaves a blessed man!
Laban pursues Jacob.
    Laban reproaches Jacob:
        What have you done?
        Why did you flee?
        Why did you not permit me?
        What have you done?
    Rachel performs a subplot:
        She hides the family gods.
        She is with her husband, against her father.
    Jacob responds in anger:
        He states his innocence.
        He recites his loyalty and hard work.
        He attests his blessing is from God,
            the God of Abraham, the Fear of Isaac.
        This God saw him!
Father-in-law and son-in-law make peace.
Laban offers a covenant of peace.
    The two agree.
    They set a boundary between them to assure disengagement.
    They mark the boundary with a pillar:
        Mizpah—watch!
        God watches!
        God maintains surveillance.
        God guarantees the boundary.
The narrative tells of mutual hostility
    and then a guarded reconciliation.

The boundary marker assures peace,
    even if not a warm peace,
    nonetheless peace.
Let the chapter be about boundaries.
    Boundaries serve to maintain distance.
    Boundaries protect the weak from the strong.
We live in a world with weak boundaries.
Empires and superpowers disregard boundaries:
    So it has been with Spain, Britain, the United States, and now Russia.
Males have had no boundaries with females;
Whites have had no boundaries with people of color.
Heterosexuals have had no boundaries with LGBTQ+ persons.
The establishment of secure boundaries is urgent in order
    to protect vulnerable populations and their resources;
    to protect females from males;
    to protect people of color from Whites;
    to protect LGBTQ+ people from predatory heterosexuals;
    to protect widows, orphans, and immigrants from the ownership class.
We may wish for and work for the overcoming of boundaries
    between Jew and Greek,
    between slave and free,
    between male and female (Gal. 3:28).
But until then, boundaries protect.
    On God's watch, boundaries are maintained;
    threats are kept under surveillance.
It is no wonder that Jacob offered a sacrifice and ate bread.

These are acts of safety and well-being
    with hostilities put on hold.
We may hope, pray, and work that our several hostilities—
    local, racial, sexual, national, global—
be kept in check by God-watched boundaries.

At our best, we appeal to you, Lord God, as the ultimate arbiter of our truth. We do not need your attestation amid our friends. But finally we turn to you amid our adversaries, as the source of truth-telling beyond all our claims. We give thanks for your utter, unwavering reliability. Amen.

ON READING GENESIS 32

And having been warned in a dream not to return to Herod,
they left for their own country by another road.

(Matt. 2:12)

Jacob is a blessed man; he has prospered.
> But he is a haunted man.
> He is haunted by his brother, Esau, whom he has cheated and deceived.

This chapter concerns the way Jacob (and all of us) continue to be haunted by our kinfolk
> whom we have left aggrieved or alienated.

Jacob must reckon with his brother, Esau, in the daytime.
> In the daytime, he is capable of careful strategic planning.
> He takes elaborately generous steps to appease his old brother whom he has injured.
> He reaches out to his brother in generosity.
> He is fearful of the abiding anger of his brother.
> He prays to the God of steadfast love and faithfulness.
>> He prays an urgent petition:
>> "Deliver me."
>
> He holds God to God's promise.
> He prepares an elaborate procession of wealth and generosity for his brother.
>> He ends the day with an emphatic "Perhaps."
>>> He hopes, but he does not know.
>>> He cannot know if his brother will accept him.
>> He has done what he could in the daylight.

Jacob must reckon with his brother all through the night.
> It is like that with our most intimate and vexed relationships.

We are preoccupied with them all day;
> we are haunted by them all night.
>> At night, he was alone;
>>> well, he thought he was alone.

But he was visited.

He wrestled all night, tossing and turning.

"A man" wrestled with him all night.
> It is like that in a nightmare;
> identities are not clear;
> nor are they constant.

Identities move in and out in our nightmares.

It was "a man."
> He has wrestled with God . . . and with man.
> Matters are fuzzy, as they always are in a nightmare.

The smiting stranger acts like God:
> He changes Jacob's name.
> He blesses him . . . .
>> Divine action!

But it is a man, almost surely Esau who haunts him all night.
> The intruder who interrupts his sleep is surely God or Esau.

Perhaps it is God who blesses;
perhaps it is Esau who haunts;
> more likely it is both.
>> Details in a nightmare are fluid and plastic and liminal.

When he awakens:

He is blessed.
> He has a new name.
>> He has seen God.
>> He has a limp.

In the daylight, he had hoped to see Esau's face;
> Now he has seen God's face
>> but has not seen Esau's face.

He is blessed,
> but nothing is resolved.

It is like that; we wrestle all night with our vexed siblings.
> We may meet God;
>> but God does not and will not resolve matters with our siblings.

So the narrative must advance.
> Jacob is left, even now, with his brother.
>> He is eager for his brother;
>> he is fearful of his brother.

We are invited to see how, in our own vexation,
> the struggle with siblings and confrontation with God are meshed together.
> At daybreak, we know this much of hard truth:
>> when we do not love our siblings whom we see,
>> we cannot love God whom we cannot see.

Jacob has seen God's face;
> it remains for him to see the face of Esau.

At bottom, we are led back to the "two great commandments":
> Love God.
> Love neighbor.
> Both meet us at night; both require engagement day after day.

We are never sure of the double vision we must face.

They always come together:
   God and Esau;
   God and brother;
   God and sibling;
   God and kinsperson;
   God and neighbor.
Two loves, two fears, two chances for reconciliation.
The day breaks.
   We, alongside Jacob, begin again
      the most durable work of reconciliation.

In our disturbed sleep, our troubled relations well up for us. Our difficult relations with our siblings get skewed and reviewed. Our dreams often end in confusion, bespeaking our lack of courage and honesty. Occupy our dreams; turn our nightmares into possibilities. Deliver us from our overimagined vulnerabilities, and let us awaken to joyous well-being. Amen.

ON READING GENESIS 33

If you remember that your brother or sister has something against you,
leave your gift there before the altar and go;
first be reconciled to your brother or sister.

(*Matt.* 5:23–24)

Now it is daybreak;
> the ambiguity of the night is shaken off.
> Jacob must deal with the reality of his brother who is before him.
> He prepares to meet him.
>> He takes precaution because he is fearful and uncertain.
>> He arranges his family in order to keep safe
>> the beloved Rachel and
>> the treasured Joseph.
>> He leads from the front.

It turns out: his fear is ungrounded.
> His brother, Esau, is no threat to him.
> Esau runs to meet him;
>> he embraces;
>>> he falls on his neck in affection;
>>>> he kisses him.
>>>>> They wept!

All is well; the procession of presentation sounds like a scene of
> Anna before Yul Brynner in *The King and I.*
> All bow before Esau in proper order and in great solemnity.

Jacob is effusive in his self-presentation to his brother.

But his brother declines; he has no need for such deference.

Jacob nonetheless responds:
> Receive me;
>> give me favor, that is, forgive me.

He alludes to the nightmare just completed:
> Seeing the face of his brother . . .
>> like seeing the face of God.

Now he has done both!
> He has seen God's face;
> he has seen the face of his brother.

Like a dramatic scene in an opera, the brothers outdo each other in performed generosity.
> Both have more than enough;
>> both have been blessed;
>>> both are eager to be seen as generous;
>> it is like a contest in generosity.

Esau looks beyond the meeting:
> he wants more time together;
>> Jacob demurs:
> too much livestock to sustain in one place.

He bids his brother to depart the meeting.
> He will follow . . . slowly . . .
>> until he catches up with him . . . he says.
> Esau wants to assure companionship;
>> he would leave some of his people with Jacob;
>>> Jacob declines.

Esau accepts Jacob's assurance.
> Why not? Both are eager to be reconciled.
> Esau departs to the desert where he belongs.

Then we notice the staggering adversative:
>> But!
> But Jacob went the other way;

but Jacob did not follow Esau slowly;
but Jacob did not do what he said.
He had declined to stay together;
he had demurred companionship with Esau;
> now we are able to see his intention all along.
>> He never intended to be together;
>> he never planned to follow his brother, slowly or otherwise;
>> he never thought to remain together.

He wanted only enough from his brother to relieve his fear;
> and now he has that relief;
>> he is safe.
> He arrives at Shechem, soon to be the site of his sons who become tribes.
> He buys a plot of land, not unlike Abraham who had purchased a burial plot.
> He possesses the land;
> he owns the land;
> he settles and worships.

The grand reconciliation is completed,
> but Jacob does not linger with it.
> He has accomplished what he needed.
> He is left unburdened,
>> having deceived his brother yet one more time.

As always with Father Jacob,
> one never knows.
> There is always a twinge of ambiguity.
> Was he honest in reconciliation
>> or only playacting?

Esau must after all have wondered:
> had he been snookered yet again?
> We wonder as well.

The narrator leaves it undecided.
It is always like that with our siblings.
We never know for sure about reconciliation.
They do not know either.
When we pretend clarity, we deceive ourselves.
The family enterprise is a cagey operation.
  We have no choice but to participate in it,
    embrace reconciliation with relief,
    sometimes with wonder,
    always with more work to do.
Thank you, God, for this singular family of promise,
  for our families, and
  for our family of faith that sustains us in our ambiguity.

Our closest relationships are quite often our most difficult and demanding tasks. You are the God who insists that we come before you reconciled people. That peacemaking work is strenuous, arduous, and long-lasting. Accompany us in that good work of forgiveness, and grant us new, unencumbered lives. Amen.

ON READING GENESIS 34

Do no wrong or violence to the alien, the orphan, and the widow, or shed innocent blood in this place.

(Jer. 22:3)

Enter Dinah,
> sister of the eleven sons of Jacob,
> only daughter of Jacob named thus far.

In this, her only narrative,
> she never acts.
> She is acted upon; she is acted for.

She is raped;
> the rapist, Shechem, loves her, wants to marry her.
> The brothers react about the rape,
>> reject his request for marriage to their sister.

But then, amid their thirst for vengeance on behalf of their sister,
> they negotiate.
> They require Shechem and his family
>> to be circumcised,
>> to become one with the family of Jacob,
>> to accept a new identity.
> Shechem accepts the terms of marriage; all parties agree.

Three days later,
> in spite of this generous accommodation
>> the brothers come and kill the offending family.

The brothers are filled with indignation, in spite of the accommodation.
> Their sister has been defiled;
> their rules of purity have been violated;

the affront to their sister (and so to them) cannot
be negotiated away;

the brothers take the required vengeance;

they kill; they seize the wealth of Shechem;

they are willing and able to act as avengers.

Thus far the narrative is as expected:

rape, indignation, vengeance, violence.

Surely a familiar tribal performance, relentless in
its resolve,

until the final verses of the chapter.

Jacob, the father of the avenging brother, father of
the raped sister, has reservations.

He sees what the violence of his sons will cost him.
The cost of vengeance to Jacob is more than he can
bear:

he is made to stink to his neighbors;

he has been made an outsider;

he is being socially rejected;

he fears an attack, worries about his own destruction.

For good reason, he rejects the vengeance wrought
by his sons.

He reprimands his sons for their eager violence,
much too costly.

His sons respond with a question:

Shall we leave her rape unanswered?

Shall we let her poor reputation stand?

Shall we forgo vengeance that is surely warranted?

Their question is left unanswered.

The narrative ends without resolution.

We are left to ponder and decide:

Shall the old violent practice of purity prevail?

Shall the pragmatism of the father override
purity?

It is a question that haunts the narrative and leaves it restless.

It is a question that haunts our contemporary world.

When is enough of destructive vengeance . . .
- between liberals and conservatives?
- between Protestants and Catholics in Ireland?
- between Israelis and Palestinians in Gaza?
- between Turks and Armenians?
- between Hindus and Muslims in India?

When is enough enough?

Father Jacob invites his sons to think again,
- to think beyond tribal indignation,
- to think practically about both past affronts and new social possibilities.

There may be an adequate response from the apostle:
- he quotes the old text wherein God declares,
- "Vengeance is mine"; that is, it is not yours.

Do not be overcome by evil, but overcome evil with good.

Faith, on the lips of Father Jacob,
- offers a heavy dose of common sense
- that may override our basest instincts.

We may wonder how the brothers answered the old quote.
- And then we may give our own answer as well,
  - an answer of wisdom, practicality, and confidence in our moral courage.

The text invites departure from old tribal instincts.
- The world waits in eager longing.

So much of our violence is domestic violence; we hurt those closest to us. Our sister Dinah may be a stand-in for all the vulnerable mothers, sisters, and daughters among us who are subject to harm and hurt. We appeal to you to be a protector of such innocent, vulnerable persons; at the same time we pledge to be attentive to such persons, to provide shelter, safety, dignity, and well-being to those who are most exposed to danger. We pray to you, God of the most exposed. Amen.

ON READING GENESIS 35

"Where, O death, is your victory?
Where, O death, is your sting?"
(1 Cor. 15:55)

This chapter gathers rich fragments from many stories.
It features Father Jacob as one
   led by God,
   responsive to God.
Jacob acknowledges
   "the God who answered me,"
   the God who revealed God's own self,
   the God who spoke a mighty promise to Jacob.
Jacob is here a pious man:
   he disposes of the foreign gods;
   he builds an altar;
   he set up a pillar;
   he offers a drink offering.
The chapter lists remembered deaths:
   Deborah, elsewhere unknown, buried and here
      remembered;
   Mother Rachel, buried and remembered,
      grieved and herself left grieving to perpetuity;
   Isaac, old and full of days,
      buried by his two sons.
Worship and death; death and worship!
What remains at the end of the chapter is the promise,
   the one concerning land and multiplicity.
We may take from this miscellany:

Worship may permeate our lives;
> Father Jacob well understood that worship
> is appropriate in every venue and every circumstance.

Death is the nonnegotiable limit of our lives; it is to be engaged, honored, and embraced
> as we treasure our dead,
> as we prepare ourselves for a good death
> > a death situated amid our faith.

What remains are the promises,
> the concrete promise of historical possibility;
> the extreme promise of fidelity,
> > or as the apostle has it:
> > > *Now abide faith, hope, and love.*

This triad may run beyond the horizon of Father Jacob,
> but the triad is tacit in his engagement with
> "the God who answered me."

It is the same God
> whom we offer worship,
> whom we trust with our deaths,
> on whom we count on in every circumstance.

We gladly confess,
> We have been answered!
> > It is always "yes."

The final threat to our life and well-being is death that remains an enigma to us. We cannot, by our technology, our science, or our faith outflank the reality of death. But we can and do rally around our conviction, "Christ is risen." We affirm, gladly and often, that death has no staying power in the face of your resolved governance of love. Amen.

ON READING GENESIS 36

*He is our peace ... [he] has broken down the dividing wall,
that is, the hostility between us.*

(Eph. 2:14)

Esau—the unchosen son—
> gets a whole chapter of forty-three verses!

The tradition has no desire to expel
> "the other brother" from its memory.
>> The tradition takes considerable effort
>>> to render "the other brother" with some specificity.

Thus "the chosen" live always with the immediacy of the "unchosen,"
> the ones who get only a second-rate blessing.

The reason for Esau's departure from the land of promise is,
> yet again,
> too much livestock in one place.

Esau functions in the tradition as a sober check
> on the assurance of being the chosen.

We Whites,
we Christians,
we White American Christians,
> are tempted, as is Israel, to pretend that we are the only ones.
> Thus we eliminate Native peoples;
> we subordinate Black peoples;
> we erase other peoples, here and abroad, as having no significance or importance.
>> Just now our political rhetoric is demeaning of all "others,"

with great imaginative passion to monopolize
the "American dream" for Whites only.
But here it is the "other,"
honored with a long-detailed genealogy,
as though every member in every generation
made some important difference.
Indeed, the Torah tradition affirms Esau as "kin" (Deut. 23:7).
Esau as "other" is a counterpoint to Ishmael as "other" (Gen. 25:12–18).
Faithful people attend to the other;
faithful people refuse exclusive White legitimacy;
faithful people allow and affirm the legitimacy of
faith among those who live outside of our
confession.
The honoring of Ishmael and then Esau is
a harbinger of the belated inclusion of "Gentiles"
in the apostolic church.
The chosen, it turns out, have no monopoly on God's goodness.
We may well ponder the belated claim that
"the middle wall of hostility"
has no lingering authority among us.
We may pray for forgiveness for our exclusion of the other,
exclusions of race,
exclusions of gender,
exclusions of class.
The good news is peace to those near at hand,
good news of peace to those far off.
The world will be healed when we see to the well-being of "the other"
and not before!

We have sins to confess;
   we have work to do;
   we have promises to share.
   Esau is a summons to the chosen to embrace the entire family.
     Thanks be to God!

Esau is the great "other" to Israel. That "other" cannot be excluded from the story of our family. And so we have a full, detailed review of the legacy of Esau. Our lives and our cultures are mightily occupied by the "other" whom we try to make invisible. But the "other" lingers. It insists on being noticed. It is part of the story we tell. We have many cousins who are not like us. You are the God of the entire family of humankind. Give us energy to be in solidarity with those whom you love as much as you love us. Amen.

ON READING GENESIS 37

"Blessed are those who mourn, for they will be comforted."
(Matt. 5:4)

"Blessed are you who weep now, for you will laugh."
(Luke 6:21)

Abruptly Joseph becomes the subject of Israel's story.
> He has, until now, rarely been mentioned, and then only incidentally.

Now he becomes central to the book of Genesis.
Joseph is the most loved, having been born late to Father Jacob.
Every family has a preferred child; here it is Joseph.
> His father, Jacob, loved him most of all;
>> He made for him special clothes.
>>> No surprise: his brothers detested him and wanted him gone.

More than that, he is a dreamer:
> He imagines the world to come with himself at its center.
> He is a spoiled child
>> who can readily place himself at the center
>> as his father had done for him.

He dreams twice:
> He dreams domination among crops . . . and they hate him!
> He dreams himself at the center of the cosmos . . . and they are jealous of him!
>> Upon hearing, Father Jacob only listens and remembers.

> He remains silent and for the moment noncommittal.

Such a dreamer is sure to evoke hostility in the family.
> It is not a surprise that his brothers want him dead.
>> Only Reuben—oldest brother—intervenes to save him.

They sold him into slavery.
> They did not kill him, but they eliminated him . . . so they thought.
>
> He is away to Egypt!
>
> Reuben—only Reuben is distressed.
>
> He is dumbfounded.
>
> He is deceived by his brothers.

Imagine: the sons of Jacob practice deception even with their oldest brother.

And then Father Jacob!
> He has lost his most beloved son.
>
> He dissolves in grief.
>
> He mourns . . . very, very deeply;
>> his loss is unbearable;
>>> his grief is beyond measure;
>>>> he refuses to be comforted.
>
> There is no comfort for a beloved son lost to violence.
>
> The father resolves to die with his unrelenting grief.

The son is sold again, a second time.
> He had been taken to Egypt;
> now he is sold to an officer of Pharaoh.

He has been placed within the oppressive regime of Pharaoh.

That he is most beloved has done him no good,
> assured him no good future.

The chapter ends in defeat for Father Jacob,
> and for the beloved of his old age.

There is here no mention of Mother Rachel in her grief;
   she is long since dead.
   But she returns in the prophetic imagination of Israel
      to weep.
   Via Jeremiah she weeps for her only child, the
      well-beloved Joseph;
      she weeps in Ramah;
      she refuses to be comforted;
      she is like her husband Jacob:
   Both father and mother refuse to be comforted.
In the prophetic oracle, Rachel is summoned by
God beyond grief into hope.
   The oracle assures return of her son;
   but for now she grieves.
She will continue to grieve in the Gospel of Matthew.
   In the imagination of Matthew, Rachel is still in
      Ramah;
   she refuses to be comforted.
Now her children are slaughtered by Herod.
   But Herod is simply Pharaoh redeployed.
   The father weeps;
   the mother weeps.
Empires and superpowers go their way in
   unrestrained violence and
   systemic exploitation.
      They easily dispose of people.
      They eliminate persons.
      They do not care.
But Israel provides this sobbing habit of weeping aloud
   that is below the radar of the empire,
   close to the ground, in the intimacy of family and
      community.
   Grief is the order of the day,

for Joseph
> and for endless uncounted victims of
> uncaring power.

The end of the chapter is unresolved.
> For now, our work is one of grief,
>> alongside Father Jacob,
>> together with Mother Rachel.

There is no ready solace,
> no easy comfort.

There is only the promise of Jeremiah, and then of Jesus:
> Blessed are those who mourn;
> they shall be comforted.

But not yet! Not for a long while yet!

The family story now moves to a new generation. That new generation, however, continues the long-running practice of violence, deception, and greed. It is no wonder that the family—our family—is narrated as a deeply conflicted enterprise that lives dangerously at the precipice of life and death. We give thanks for your hovering grace that provides us enough stamina to pursue the destiny you have entrusted to us. Amen.

ON READING GENESIS 38

"God, I thank you that I am not like other people:
thieves, rogues, adulterers, or even like this tax collector."
(Luke 18:11)

The narrative of Joseph pauses
   long enough to host the story of Judah.
The chapter concerns sustenance of the family line
   that will lead to David
   and eventually to Jesus.
That continuity of the family line is mediated through irregular and deceptive actions.
   The irregularity and deception come as no surprise;
   they are the hallmark of Jacob and his family.
The story revolves around Tamar, a Canaanite.
   The ancestral narrative cannot dispense with outsiders;
   they are repeatedly essential to the plot.
The intrigue enacted by Tamar is evoked by
   the death of the sons of Judah
   and her requirement of a father in order to produce an heir.
Tamar, the Canaanite, takes daring steps outside of normal protocol
   to secure a father for the child she must have.
Tamar wants a productive mate;
   Judah wants only the satisfaction of a prostitute.
   In her cunning, Tamar secures evidence of their liaison . . . just in case.
   Upon hearing of the role of a prostitute,

Judah is filled with righteous indignation . . .
 until he discerns his own culpability.
Judah makes no excuse for himself;
 he acknowledges Tamar;
 he commends her; she is "more righteous."
The heir of the chosen is birthed by the Canaanite.
Her linkage to Judah produces twins:
 One, Zerah, is sloughed off by the narrative;
 the other, Perez, activates the family line
  that leads to David and,
   in Christian tradition, to Jesus.
 The narrative can memorialize both Tamar and Perez
  as keys to the royal genealogy.
The story depends upon the wiles of a woman who must make her way in a man's world.
The story depends upon a Canaanite who keeps the royal line of Israel intact.
The story depends upon the courageous deception through which Judah is made hostage enough for blackmail.
What a revolutionary culmination:
 a woman outflanking a man;
 a Canaanite overwhelming an Israelite;
 a deception that perpetuates faith.
What a verdict: "She is more righteous."
We may ponder the use of "righteous."
The term here cannot mean obedience to commandments;
 it cannot mean adherence to norms;
  it cannot mean conventional virtue.
Rather "more righteous" may mean
 a greater contribution to the well-being of the community,

even with moral corner-cutting.
The story is profoundly subversive.
> It undermines all conventionality.
>
> Happily, Judah, carrier of the family line,
> > could embrace the Canaanite subverter,
> >
> > even as the story exposes him.

God's way into the future is one reliant on complex, compromised human action.
> The defining purpose of God is kept
> > but not in "regular order."

We may attend to this chapter carefully,
> because it attests to faith as the practice of real people in the real world.

The underside of the text invites us to be more
> attentive to the underside of our own lived reality.

The text is an invitation for the church to break out of its "niceness"
> in order to see how our "mixed evidence" may host the God of abiding fidelity.

All praise to such a resourceful, risk-taking God
> who keeps us in, with, and under our complexity.

We "good people" dare to come into your presence with excessive self-confidence. We are always again surprised that our good credentials do not score with you. We see in your generous reach a special concern for the unqualified, unsuccessful, and unrighteous. Give us mercy to revamp our ways of knowing and perceiving the world that you love. Amen.

ON READING GENESIS 39

> *Do not fear, for I have redeemed you;*
> *I have called you by name, you are mine.*
> *(Isa. 43:1)*

Joseph has been sold twice and ends in Egypt.
He is now the property of an officer of the Egyptian Pharaoh.
We get three distinct moments in this chapter.
First, Joseph is blessed;
   He has immense success.
   The Lord is with him.
      The power of God on his behalf is hidden, but nonetheless powerful.
         Joseph readily rises to the top . . . in charge of all!
Second, Joseph is handsome, good-looking, enormously attractive.
   He is a sexual temptation.
      He is pursued by the wife of his owner . . . a sure danger.
   She cannot resist him.
   He refuses her:
      great wickedness against God;
      he has a clear moral compass, plus an awareness of the risks.
         He would have readily embraced the seventh commandment of Moses's Torah.
         Such sex is a no-no of serious proportion.
But she persists, wants sex with him.
   He refuses yet again.

Embarrassed, she sets him up and accuses him.
> She identifies him only as "a Hebrew,"
>> a lowly presence without identity, territorial or political location . . . most vulnerable.

She justifies her accusation: The Hebrew insulted me.
> Not an insult . . . a refusal!
> Enough to impact her self-regard.

She will punish him for his refusal,
> for his stance of honor.

It is an old story of high-placed women pursuing vulnerable men,
> an old story in our society of White women who exploit vulnerable Black men.

Third, Joseph is framed.
> He is punished by imprisonment.
>> Justice works quickly for the powerful:
>>> no trial, no investigation,
>>> only "she said" in her accusation.

The narrative ends with a defining, defiant conjunction: BUT!

But YHWH was with him.

But YHWH showed him *hesed*.
> This claim from the beginning is reiterated and reinforced.
>
> He found favor yet again, this time from his jailor.

This chapter twice features a stunning juxtaposition:
> YHWH was with him . . . "Hebrew."

At the outset, he is successful because the Lord was with him.

At the end, Joseph prospers because the Lord was with him.

In between, the wife of Potiphar twice reports:
> A *Hebrew* insulted us.

The *Hebrew* servant insulted me.
The Lord is with lowliest, most despised Joseph;
   here he is not an "Israelite" but only a mere "Hebrew"
     without any claim of any kind.
God is in solidarity with the lowliest.
   This juxtaposition is, among other things, an anticipation of Paul's triad:
     God chose what is foolish in the world;
     God chose what is weak in the world;
     God chose what is low and despised in the world.
Or in the words of Jesus:
   the last will be first;
   the humble will be exalted.
We may pray for the will and capacity to see
   among the foolish, weak, low, and despised
   your powerful governance.
Pray we will notice more than did the beguiled wife of Potiphar.

We thank you that you regularly turn your attention to those who are left out and left behind. We give thanks for your steadfast love that violates the ways of ordered society and that tilts toward those without power or leverage. Free us from any illusion that our well-being stems from our merit, that we may trust in and rely on you in your immeasurable capacity for fidelity. Amen.

ON READING GENESIS 40

So the last will be first.
(Matt. 20:16)

Joseph has affronted an officer of Pharaoh;
  he is in prison with two officials of Pharaoh,
    the chief cupbearer, the chief baker.
Dreams beset the two of them,
  as they restlessly generate futures for themselves.
    Their dreams bewilder:
    They cannot decipher them.
    They need an interpreter of their dreams.
  Joseph willingly plays the role of dream interpreter;
    he is the all-purpose manager, loaded with competence.
The chief cupbearer dreams a dream;
  Joseph interprets:
    Restoration!
    Rehabilitation!
    Head lifted up!
  Joseph, himself a prisoner, asks of the cupbearer,
    remember me,
    do me *hesed*,
    mention my name to Pharaoh.
The chief baker dreams a dream;
  Joseph interprets:
    Bad news!
    Head lifted off,
    prey for the birds.
Resolution: a third day restoration!
  Cupbearer: head lifted up;

Baker: hanged, head lifted off.
Pharaoh is all-powerful—end of chapter—end of story.
Joseph, forgotten and neglected, lingers in prison.
He is helpless before the power of Pharaoh,
> Except ... we know ...
>> he has the power of dream interpretation;
> he has power that may outdistance the force of Pharaoh.

Pharaoh can manage his world;
> but there is another world he cannot manage,
>> one to which he has no access.

We will watch and wait;
> we will see how the dreamer,
> the one who interprets,
>> presides over the future.

His gifts might have put Pharaoh on notice,
> except that Pharaoh—as always—is unnoticing.
> But we notice.
>> We pay attention to the wondrous, demanding reality outside the domain of Pharaoh.

This is governance from "elsewhere," not of this world.

We are skilled in forgetting what we should remember and in remembering what we should forget. Give us the gift of attentiveness that we may notice the ways in which we have prospered through the efforts of others. Deliver us from any illusion of self-sufficiency. We take every gesture of support and sustenance as a sign of a more excellent way in the world. Amen.

ON READING GENESIS 41

*For which of you, intending to build a tower, does not first sit down
and estimate the cost, to see whether he has enough to complete it? ...
Or what king, going out to wage war against another king, will not
sit down first and consider whether he is able with ten thousand to
oppose the one who comes against him with twenty thousand?*
(Luke 14:28, 31)

More dreams!
More need for the dream interpreter.
    Pharaoh is all-powerful;
    but he cannot prevent the intrusion of this other
        world beyond his control.
Pharaoh dreams twice:
    fat cows / lean, ugly cows;
    plump grain / blighted grain.
There is no competent Egyptian dream interpreter;
    that art is withheld from the empire;
        but
    there is this "young Hebrew" ... still in prison.
Joseph is summoned by Pharaoh ... out of prison!
The dreams are reiterated.
Joseph, by the working of God, readily interprets
what had stymied the Egyptians:
    seven good cows / seven good ears = seven years
        of plenty;
    seven ugly cows / seven blighted ears = seven
        years of famine.
This is "from God"; Pharaoh is helpless before it.
    Pharaoh's governance is quite penultimate,
    as Joseph attests.

Joseph does not pause; he promptly turns from dream to response:
"now therefore."
The interpreter becomes the planner:
needed: one wise and discerning,
one capable of organizing,
one to shape and lead policy,
one capable of storing up abundance.
The knowing Egyptians nominate Joseph to lead the abundance . . .
wise and discerning.
Joseph receives exalted authorization:
the prisoner has become the governor;
he is installed as food czar;
he gets the ring from Pharaoh;
he gets fine linen;
he gets an ornate chain;
he gets his own chariot, plus public adulation.
He is "over all";
he is in charge.
This abrupt reversal is the truth of the story.
The inversion for Joseph is the work of the God "with him."
This is the characteristic, recurring work of God,
the one who frees the enslaved,
the one who returned the exiles,
the one who evoked new Easter life,
the one who makes new,
"who forgives all your iniquity,
who heals all your diseases,
who redeems your life from the Pit,
who crowns you with steadfast love and mercy,

> who satisfies you with good as long as you
> live . . .
> [who] works vindication
> and justice for all who are oppressed." (Ps.
> 103:3–6).

The narrator does not explain, unable to explain;
> the narrator can only tell the story,
> > bear witness to inexplicable newness,
> > the same newness for widows, orphans, and immigrants,
> > the same newness for the blind, the deaf, the lepers, the poor, the dead.
> Joseph's abrupt rise to power attests to the wild card of God
> > whose governance is well beyond the reckoning of Pharaoh.

Joseph, as expected, is fully competent;
> he gathered the food supply;
> he stored up the food beyond measure.

He is the wave of the future,
> thus his two sons,
> > Manasseh . . . forget hardship,
> > Ephraim . . . fruitful.
> > > Sons to specify the inexplicable will of God.

The famine came, as per the dream;
> but Pharaoh is ready;
> Egypt had ample food;
> Joseph prevailed.

The erstwhile prisoner is a harbinger of
emancipation yet to come.
We may wonder how it is
> that good resources happen well beyond
> > our governance,

>> our control,
>> our knowledge,
>> our technology.

Indeed, our faith is a meditation upon and a practice of this inscrutable reality.

It is enough to ponder that Pharaoh's mighty rule is never ultimate,
> ample reason for gratitude and for alternative obedience.

We thank you for the capacity among us to plan wisely for the use of our resources. We are grateful for smart, knowledgeable people who know how to organize resources for the common good. We are chagrined at those who use such skills in order to accumulate for themselves or to utilize common resources for private gain. We pray (and hope and plan) for the common good that you intend among us. Amen.

ON READING GENESIS 42

> *"The LORD indeed will be with you,*
> *if ever I let your little ones go with you!"*
> *(Exod. 10:10)*

This chapter begins the long process of four chapters of reconciliation for Joseph with his brothers:
> It is a slow, carefully choreographed enterprise
> > that comes as one dramatic effort.

The context is famine;
> it will only become more severe.

The attraction is Egypt,
> the land of ample grain —
> > due to the forethought of Joseph!

The action in this chapter is like a carefully staged drama.
> Joseph is the lead character,
> > as cagey and manipulative as was his father.
> The brothers are an unwitting counterpoint to their powerful brother.

Joseph is harsh and demanding,
> willing to test his brothers,
> aiming all the time to see his younger brother, Benjamin.

The brothers are tricked and trapped by the cleverness of their brother.
> He demands delivery of the young Benjamin;
> the brothers are smitten with guilt and
> are rendered helpless before the powerful governor
> > whom they do not recognize as their brother.

The contest proceeds

with Joseph fully aware,
the brothers unknowing and uncomprehending.
At first Joseph will keep nine of his brothers hostage
and send one home to fetch Benjamin.
Then Joseph relents, keeps only one brother, Simeon, as hostage.
    Reuben stands out, yet again, as the one brother with some sensibility.
Joseph is surreptitiously generous;
    he returns the money to his brothers;
    he gives the grain to them along with their money;
    the grain is free, from his ample storage.
The brothers, minus Simeon,
    return home.
        They have grain;
        they have their money back;
        they are panic-stricken,
            for they do not and cannot understand what has happened to them.
        The work is that of Joseph;
        they take it rather as God's providence.
        God has done this!
We finish with Father Jacob;
    he remains at home;
    he remains in deep grief;
    he has lost beloved Joseph;
        now they want favored Benjamin as well.
    He refuses;
    he will not trade his young son for grain.
Yet again, oldest son Rueben steps in to offer an assurance;
    Father Jacob refuses, Benjamin alone is left!
Our chapter ends in a stalemate—

the bargain on offer
a *son* for *grain* . . .
grain for a *son*.

The Egyptian governor is not serious;
> he is playacting in a hidden way;
> but the father and brothers do not know this.

We end without resolution.
> It is the kind of stalemate we see
> > wherever hostages are taken,
> > wherever political force dominates human reality.

We are left with the question of Father Jacob:
> How much is a son worth?
> He answers: my young son is worth everything.

We may be haunted in our world of violence and hostage taking:
> What is the life of a child worth?
> It is the question Father Abraham had to ask at Mt. Moriah;
> in Christian tradition, it is a Friday question posed for our Heavenly Father.
> It is a question now on offer in many places,
> > not least in Gaza!

Joseph speaks for many parents who refuse to bargain their children.

For now, Joseph's cleverness has prevailed.
> Israel as of now has no sure supply of grain;
> we await the next episode;

we wait alongside our precious children who cannot be bargained or traded;
it is a torturous wait.

You are the protector of orphans and of all vulnerable children. The economy of Pharaoh among us denies the value of children and uses them as pawns in the contest for money and power. We know better, because every child matters in your purview. Grant that we may be advocates and guarantors for every vulnerable child, assuring each one the dignity and security that is their birthright. Amen.

ON READING GENESIS 43

The wolf shall live with the lamb,
the leopard shall lie down with the kid,
the calf and the lion and the fatling together,
and a little child shall lead them.
                    (Isa. 11:6)

The slow drama of reconciliation continues.
Context: severe famine.
Reality: Egypt has abundant grain.
At the outset,
   son Judah remonstrates with Father Jacob;
     he wants to return to Egypt;
     he wants to take young Benjamin with him.
     His urgency: he wants to keep his own "little ones" safe from the famine;
     he will not go without his brother Benjamin,
       or risk his life before Joseph.
In response,
   Father Jacob, albeit with reluctance, agrees and grants permission to Judah.
   The father loads up his son with tasty gifts for the prime minister:
   balm,
     honey,
       gum,
         resin,
           pistachio nuts,
            almonds,
   all rich food designed to impress and persuade.
The father commends his emissary son to El Shaddai.

It is all against his better judgment,
> but his hand is forced.

At the sight of Benjamin,
> the powerful prime minister prepares a lavish dinner for his guests.
>
> He reveals nothing.

The brothers are assured by—of all people—Joseph's steward,
> "the man over the house."
>
> The steward responds with assurance;
> > what they fear is indeed the work of God,
> > "your God and the God of your father."
>
> We get hints of the hidden work of providence;
> > even the Egyptian steward can attest the God who moves in mysterious ways.
>
> All is ready for the celebrative meal.

Joseph is moved by the sight of Benjamin,
> his only brother born to Rachel.
>
> > He weeps, but in private.
> >
> > High government officials do not cry in public.
> >
> > (Ask Senator Edmund Muskie, who wept in public and had to end his campaign.)

Still nothing revealed!
> They eat,
> but not together.
>
> > Egyptians do not and cannot eat with low-class Hebrews;
> > > it is an abomination, not unlike Whites eating with Blacks during Jim Crow!

What a mouthful: Joseph is an Egyptian with their eating habits!
> He has all the trappings of Egyptian power;
> he has all the marks of Egyptian identity;

he will not show himself otherwise,
he stays "in role."
The brothers eat alone,
without their Egyptian benefactor;
but the prime minister attends to detail;
Benjamin, young treasured Benjamin,
gets five times as much!
He is lavished with royal abundance;
he is the star of the drama;
he is risked by Father Jacob;
he is protected by his brother Judah;
he is the one now seen by his brother, Joseph.
But the tension is not yet relieved.
The narrative crisis is not yet resolved;
the brothers may have enjoyed their meal,
but they must be on their guard.
Negotiations between the powerful and the powerless are inescapably tricky and dangerous.
It is like negotiations between White predators and Native Americans;
it is like negotiations between White owners and erstwhile enslaved Black persons;
it is like every one-sided negotiation;
it requires moral courage;
it demands running risks.
Meanwhile the meal is extravagant.
The brother prime minister,
the one identified as an Egyptian,
must have enjoyed the scene.
He delighted in managing the party;
he deceived his brothers;
he has in his imperial way prevailed . . . for now.
Beyond the "for now" of Joseph,

the Egyptian steward has put us on notice:
God is at work here. Here is another verse of the hymn "God Moves in a Mysterious Way":

"Judge not the Lord by feeble sense,
But trust him for his grace,
Behind a frowning providence,
He hides a smiling face."

It takes the witness of an Egyptian to remind us that this narrative —
like all of our narratives —
includes the hidden force of holiness.
It is a hidden force that makes all else penultimate.

Imagine Benjamin . . . young, innocent, and vulnerable! Nonetheless he becomes the gate through which food can flow from Pharaoh to the needy family of Jacob. We give thanks for Benjamin and for all our children in their innocent vulnerability. Teach us to rely on the innocence of our children that can counter the force of fear among us adults. Let us be on the watch for such vulnerable conduits of shared well-being. Amen.

ON READING GENESIS 44

> *Wait for the LORD; be strong,*
> *and let your heart take courage;*
> *wait for the LORD.*
>   *(Ps. 27:14)*

Joseph remains hidden from his brothers.
Now he engages in yet one more ruse.
  He instructs his steward;
  he dispatches his steward;
  he provides four questions his steward is to ask:
    ????
  He convicts his brothers of wrong.
His brothers plead innocent of his charges;
  they invite a search of their sacks;
  the outcome of the search:
    Benjamin!
  The one most cherished and most protected is guilty!
  The prime minister wants only Benjamin!
In response to the ruse of the prime minister,
  Judah voices a long, extended petition.
    He has sworn to protect his younger brother;
    he reviews the exchange he had with his fearful, reluctant father;
    he petitions the prime minister:
      let the boy return home;
      save our father from suffering.
In this chapter, Judah's appeal remains unanswered;
  Joseph does not respond.

The chapter attests the complexity of the interaction
of the brothers:
> it exhibits Joseph in his deception;
>
> it presents Judah in his great anxiety;
>
> it offers Benjamin in his vulnerability.

The drama of the brothers is complex and filled
with angst.

The tension among siblings goes unrelieved.

Some of the most demanding, most disturbing issues
> concern those closest at hand,
>
> the ones we are assigned to love,
>
> the ones who can most readily trigger negativity.

We are left with the old question:
> Am I my brother's keeper?
>
> It is a question asked by Judah —
>> he knows the answer is "yes."
>>
>> Yes, you must answer for your brother.
>
> It is a question asked by Joseph;
>> he knows the answer is "yes"; but he restrains
>> himself.

At the moment, the young vulnerable Benjamin
> remains a pawn in the manipulation of the prime
> minister.

Like many such complexities among siblings,
> the matter is unresolved;
>
> the narrator makes us wait:
>> Judah must wait;
>>
>> Jacob must wait;
>>
>> Benjamin must wait.

It is a long wait . . . with an uncertain outcome.

It is like that with siblings:
> Long wait . . . no sure outcome or resolution.

Our world is fraught with unresolved sibling rivalries:

Catholics and Protestants in Ireland;
Jews and Palestinians in Gaza;
Hindus and Muslims in India.
> etc., etc., etc.

In our chapter, we may think the matter is in God's hand;
> except that the prime minister has the strong hand.
> As often, the outcome depends on the reach of the more powerful.

The narrative does not blink at holding the matter in unrelieved tension.
> We, along with Judah, must wait in long lingering.
> At best, the narrator—and God—makes haste only slowly.
>> We may be grateful for our capacity to wait, albeit impatiently.

We are not in the habit of waiting; we want what we want when we want it. But we learn, soon or late, to live at your pace. You are "unresting, unhasting, and silent as light." Give us patience to live at your pace wherein a "thousand ages . . . are like an evening gone."[1] Give us readiness to wait in anticipation for your way in the world. We wait and hope in eager longing, ready to receive the gifts you give us in your slow-moving generosity. Amen.

---

1. The quotations in the prayer are from "Immortal, Invisible, God Only Wise" and "O God, Our Help in Ages Past."

ON READING GENESIS 45

He satisfies the thirsty,
and the hungry he fills with good things.
(Ps. 107:9)

Finally . . .
  finally the truth is told;
  finally Joseph breaks his deception and identifies
    himself;
  finally the brothers receive his reliable assurance;
  finally the future is open for Jacob and his family;
  finally the reconciliation is accomplished.
  Finally . . . for all we have waited.
Joseph's restraint has reached its limit;
  he can fake it no longer.
  He reveals himself:
    "I am Joseph."
    I am your brother;
    I am the one whom you sold into slavery.
(This self-declaration was belatedly echoed by John
XXIII as he drew closer to Jewish believers;
  he declared himself to be "Joseph your brother.")
Joseph reveals the agenda of the narrator:
  God sent me before you.
  God sent me before you;
  God has made me a father to Pharaoh;
  God has made me lord of Egypt:
    it was not happenstance;
    it was not his achievement;
    it was "the God who provides,"
      the God who sees ahead of time,

> the God of pro-video.
>> the same God who provided the lamb for Abraham at Mt. Moriah.
>
> The world—the brothers, Pharaoh, Egypt—
>> all are held in the hidden hand of God.
>>> "God has all threads firmly in his hands
>>>> Even when men are least aware of it."[2]
>
> Joseph moved easily from affirmation to imperative:
>> Come down to me;
>> do not delay;
>> settle in Goshen;
>> be near me;
>>> I will provide all for you there; no poverty!
>> Hurry!
>>> Oh yes, Benjamin!
>> He draws the attention of the prime minister
>>> who wept and kissed and wept.
>
> Pharaoh issues a big welcome to the family of Jacob.
>> Imagine, mighty Pharaoh attending to this family of fugitives!
>>> Pharaoh loads wagons with goods;
>>> he sends transport;
>>> he offers good land;
>>> he exhibits boundless generosity;
>>> he reiterates and reinforces the anticipation of Joseph;
>>> nothing is too good or too much for the family of his much-trusted prime minister.
>
> Now the family of Jacob—of Abraham and of Isaac—
>> is hosted by Pharaoh

---

2. Gerhard von Rad, *The Problem of the Hexateuch and Other Essays* (McGraw Hill, 1966), 297.

and dwells in the land of Pharaoh.
Joseph parallels the generosity of Pharaoh:
  he sends wagons;
  he sends garments.
    Beloved Benjamin gets more:
      much silver plus five sets of garments,
        highly privileged!
Joseph sends donkeys loaded with provisions.
  Joseph and Pharaoh together break all limits of generosity on behalf of this chosen family!
The brothers return home to Canaan;
  they report to their father:
    Joseph is alive!
    He governs Egypt!
The old father is stunned and unbelieving;
  he sees the wagons loaded with generosity.
  He is revived!
    "Enough!" (In Hebrew, "much still added again.")
    His son is alive!
    He must see him!
For now, the old man is indifferent to all the lavish goods;
  he only wants his son;
  he must see him;
  he must go to him;
  it is the craving of his life . . . now it comes to pass.
Jacob and his family are guests of Pharaoh;
  they do not fear Pharaoh . . . yet;
  they are not on notice about Pharaonic power . . . yet!
  They do not sense any risk for themselves at the hand of Pharaoh . . . yet!
We, along with Jacob,
  may be grateful for the largess of the ownership class;

> we may be appreciative when wealth and power serve need;
>
> we, along with Jacob, are on our way, rejoicing at the happy turn of events.

The father has a dead son now alive.
> It is an anticipation of the father in the parable who will sing and dance:

"This brother of yours was dead and has come to life; he was lost and has been found." (Luke 15:32)

We may imagine that other Father

—on Easter morning—

glad that his only begotten Son is alive,

back in the world

> to do the good work of emancipation and reconciliation.

So much to celebrate as Father Jacob sets out!

You are the great provider! You provide what we need for our life. Your generous provisions come to us through willing, able human agents who know how to manage and administer the gifts you give. We give thanks for wise planners of food production and distribution and the good administrators who plan well. Deliver us from policies of greed and from agents of accumulation, that we may commonly share in the good gifts you give. Amen.

ON READING GENESIS 46

*Therefore they set taskmasters over them to oppress them with
   forced labor.*
They built supply cities, Pithom and Rameses, for Pharaoh.
   (Exod. 1:11)

Jacob will not depart for Egypt
  before he is given a promise by God:
  it is God who will make Jacob a great nation . . .
     there . . . in Egypt;
  it is God who will bring Israel out again.
  In this utterance the voice of God bespeaks the
     governing plot of Israel's faith:
        into Egypt . . . out of Egypt!
With the promise of God in hand, Father Jacob
loaded up his enormous wealth;
  he gathered his family for the journey to the land
     of Pharaoh.
The narrative pauses to give us a complete index of
the traveling family.
  It is a huge enterprise —
  all the brothers and their wives and offspring,
     seventy in all!
Of note:
  Dinah, his daughter, goes with the family,
     the one who had been shamed
     and then had her honor restored by her violent
        brothers;
  Manasseh and Ephraim, born to Joseph,
     birthed by an Egyptian mother!

They are all ready;
>they all set out;
>they all travel . . . to Egypt;
>they arrive in Goshen . . . good pasture land.
>The father meets his long-lost son;
>>the son arrives with the majesty of his Egyptian chariot; his honor on exhibit.
>The father does not care, is not impressed by the royal pomp;
>he sees only his son, the one he has lost.
>He weeps, his hope fulfilled;
>>his life complete . . . ready to die!

The chapter ends with the appearance of Pharaoh, who settles them in good pasture land.
>It will not take very long for Egypt to sour for the family of Jacob
>>. . . a new Pharaoh!

But for now,
>well-being,
>>safety,
>>>security,
>>>>abundance!

The plotline exhibits a God who keeps promises.
>The line continues;
>the promise persists;
>the hope abides.

In Christian venue, that hope goes like this:
>"Standing on the promises of Christ my King,
>through eternal ages let his praises ring;
>glory in the highest, I will shout and sing,
>standing on the promises of God.
>Standing, standing,
>standing on the promises of God my Savior;

standing, standing,
I'm standing on the promises of God."³

In Jewish horizon,
it may be the holy land of promise,
or it may be a Torah-ordered world of justice and mercy.

The narrator pauses and makes us, along with the family of Jacob, wait.

New prospects are under way!

You put your special people in a circumstance of inequity and risk where the food supply is controlled by the force of empire. We do not understand why you establish such threatening inequality or why you permit human agents to monopolize in greed. We give thanks for your gift of food and pray its abundance for all the hungry, most of whom are powerless in the world. Amen.

---

3. R. Kelso Carter, "Standing on the Promises," in *The United Methodist Hymnal* (The United Methodist Publishing House, 1989), #374.

ON READING GENESIS 47

Do not let the wise boast in their wisdom, do not let the mighty boast in their might, do not let the wealthy boast in their wealth; but let those who boast boast in this, that they understand and know me, that I am the LORD; I act with steadfast love, justice, and righteousness in the earth, for in these things I delight.

(Jer. 9:23–24)

Finally we get this dramatic meeting . . .
   the mighty king and the old chieftain.
   The mighty king is generous;
      he assigns land to the needy shepherds.
We might expect Pharaoh to bless the old man from his largesse;
   but we get role reversal:
      Jacob blesses Pharaoh . . . twice.
   Jacob is filled with the power to bless;
      he has ample power to bless;
      he bestows the power of his blessing upon the
         Egyptian king.
Jacob knows who he is;
   where he belongs;
      to whom he belongs as a carrier of blessing.
But not Joseph!
   Joseph is unlike his father;
      he has an Egyptian office and authority;
      he has an Egyptian wife;
      he has an Egyptian chariot;
      he has an Egyptian ring on his finger;
      he has an Egyptian gold chain around his neck;
      he has fine-linen Egyptian garments.

And now—we discover—
> he thinks like one at the head of empire;
>> he has inhaled the ideology of Pharaoh;
>>> his policy (and perhaps his entire life) is all about "more";
>>> more grain, more money, more control, more power . . . never enough yet!

His work is in a Pharaonic mode.
James C. Scott has taught us the wonder of grain for ancient monopolists:
> Grain can be stored; it can be transported;
> it is the perfect, most reliable form of wealth in the ancient world;
> social security depends on a monopoly of grain![4]

Joseph, the powerful Egyptian (!) ruler, plays monopoly;
> he will not stop until he has a monopoly;
> he collects all the grain;
> he sells the grain;
> he trades the grain for livestock;
> he trades the grain for land;
> he trades the grain . . . finally . . . for the lives of the peasants;
>> he makes them his slaves;
> they are glad to be his slaves; he saved them!

Joseph, the Egyptian, possessed the land, the livestock, the grain, the slaves,
> everything on which he could get his hands.

He is so unlike his father, Jacob!
And then the end comes for the old man;

---

4. James C. Scott, *Against the Grain: A Deep History of the Earliest States* (Yale University Press, 2018).

he wants to be sure to be buried properly;
he knows his right place;
he wants to come down where he ought to be;
he does not trust his wily son;
he makes sure by the most demanding oath
- to be buried in the right place, in the land of promise.

He knows what the promise holds for him and his posterity.

This chapter has as its subject
- *Identity:* Jacob knew who he was, and
- *Ideology:* Joseph embraced a phony identity, one defined by his property.

We live in a culture of great ideological seduction:
- It is easy enough to fall into an ideology of White nationalism,
  - as if our identity was given us in a political faction, or conversely,
- it is easy enough to fall into an ideology of urban technology remote from natural reality,
  - as if our identity was to be equated with our self-sufficiency.

We face twin (maybe more!) powerful ideologies,
- White nationalism/
  - urban technology.
- Each promises security, well-being, identity;
  - both are phony.

The alternative to ideology is rootage in a tradition of promise,
- wherein our identity and our life is given us,
- promises kept alive by the faith of Israel.
  - The struggle for genuine identity as a beloved creature of God

is a demanding task in our society.
This is a chance to escape the grip of ideology;
> it is genuine existence as a child of God,
>> a life that comes from God
>> and answers back to God.

In Judaism, a mark of that genuine identity is circumcision,
> a son of the promise;

In Christian faith, the mark of genuine identity is baptism
> wherein we are marked as "Christ's own forever."

Our narrative offers us a stark contrast between
> the father who knows who he is and
> the son who mistakenly identifies himself through his possessions.
>> The father wishes it were otherwise for his son, but it could not be;
>> the force of Pharaoh is too great for Joseph;
>>> he counts too heavily on his ideological props.

Finally the father must rest his head.
> He trusts the identity given him by the God of promises.
> He will stand on the promises,
>> while his son exults in his worldly success.

It was such a dramatic confrontation: the mighty ruler of empire in all his powerful regalia and the old man who came with only his faith. We are always in this confrontation between the force of "this age" and the truth that moves in and through it. Give us courage and wisdom for such confrontation, that we may not fail to recognize where our true future is on offer. Amen.

ON READING GENESIS 48

> *"Then LORD makes poor and makes rich;*
> *he brings low, he also exalts.*
> *He raises up the poor from the dust;*
> *he lifts the needy from the ash heap,*
> *to make them sit with princes*
> *and inherit a seat of honor."*
> *(1 Sam. 2:7–8)*

Father Jacob is a feeble old man;
> we have just left him with his head on his bed;
> but he is not finished yet.

He reiterates for his beloved son, Joseph, the long-running promise of land and progeny.
> He adopts as his own the two sons of Joseph,
>> Ephraim and Manasseh.
>>> Joseph silently complies with his father's arbitrary wish.
>
> Thus the two sons of Joseph join the roster of Jacob's own sons.
>
> Jacob remembers that the two are the grandsons of beloved Rachel;
> he draws them near.

In his feeble blindness,
> he adopts his two grandsons, now as his own;
> he kisses them;
> he embraces them.
>
> He will bless them.
>
> The two are aligned so that the right hand of the grandfather,
>> the strong hand,

will be on the head of the older, Manasseh.
At the last moment, old Jacob plays one more trick
in his long-running trickery.
He crosses his arms!
His right hand of power reached for Ephraim, the younger;
his other hand, less powerful, is left for the older, Manasseh.
His action is inexplicable;
it is also irreversible!
Jacob blesses his own son Joseph
and his two grandsons now adopted.
He blesses the boys
that they may be safe and multiply;
they are both blessed.
Joseph is on the alert during this action by his father.
He sees that his old father has crossed his arms.
He has extended his powerful right hand to the second son;
Joseph protests;
he supports regular order;
he assumes primogeniture.
The old man is wistful, as though he could not help himself;
as though to say, "I know, I know, my bad."
There is a moment of arm wrestling:
his son tries to uncross the arms of the old man;
the father refuses and lets his act stand.
We are not told why;
perhaps Jacob remembers his deception of his brother, Esau, and reperforms that travesty;
perhaps he is cunning in his old age and enjoys the game;

perhaps the action is destined by God.
   We are not told.
      Either way, his trickery continues;
         the birth order is inverted.
The old man has one more blessing
   for both grandsons.
   As a final gesture, he gives a double portion to Joseph, his favorite.
The chapter—and the future—depends
   upon this reversal of "regular order" done without explanation.
The Bible—and the God of the Bible—refuse what we easily take to be "regular order."
Jacob is, to the end, a trickster;
   even more, God is a trickster!
In the long run, God's subversion prevails:
   the first last, the last first;
   the humble exalted; the exalted humbled;
   weakness stronger than strength;
   foolishness wiser than wisdom;
   poverty richer than wealth!
We are left off-balance by the subversion of this trickster God.
We may imagine ourselves arm wrestling with God,
   trying to uncross God's arms;
   seeking to preserve and protect "natural order."
   We may imagine God responding wistfully,
      "I know, my child, I know.
      I could not help myself."

You are the God who intrudes upon our social arrangements. Just when we had matters all settled to our advantage, you stir the pot, evoke energy from below, and evoke change that we do not welcome. Give us the courage to recognize that we are penultimate and that you are the sure and ultimate arbiter of our way in the world. You are the dealer of the wild card. We thank you for the cunning of Father Jacob who echoes your own cunning will. Amen.

ON READING GENESIS 49

> *I am distressed for you, my brother Jonathan;*
> *greatly beloved were you to me;*
> *your love to me was wonderful,*
> *passing the love of women.*
>
> (2 Sam. 1:26)

The old father is fresh from his trickster blessing of his two adopted grandsons.
   Now, in a highly stylized way,
      he blesses all his sons.
   His blessings are arbitrary, without any reason given.
   He anticipates and seeks to impact the futures of
      his sons-become-tribes.
   He has ample authority and force to do such a blessing,
      some of which turn out to be curses.
Of the four early sons of Leah,
   he dismisses three of them:
      Reuben, Simeon, and Levi.
   Of the four, only Judah is generously blessed.
   The old man anticipates "the scepter" for Judah,
      that is, King David to come from the line of Judah.
   Judah will receive tribute;
      he will receive obedience;
         he will prevail.
Of the belated sons born to Leah,
   Zebulun will be by the sea,
   Issachar will have good pasture land,
      both are blessed, only briefly.
Of the two sons born to Zilpah, maid of Leah

the future will be good,
>   Gad to be a raider,
>   Asher to eat royal delicacies.
>   Jacob does not linger over them.

Of the two sons born to Bilhah, maid to Rachel,
>   Dan is dismissed as a snake,
>   Naphtali is affirmed as a doe with beautiful fawns,
>   both voiced briefly.

Of the two sons born to Rachel,
>   Benjamin will be a devouring wolf,
>   but Joseph …
>   much blessed,
>   blessed by the mighty one,
>   blessed by the shepherd,
>   blessed by the Rock of Israel,
>   blessed by the God of your father,
>   blessed by El Shaddai,
>   blessed by the deep,
>   blessed by the breasts and the womb,
>   blessed by your father,
>   completely blessed!

Each son a suitable blessing . . . or curse.
>   The two winners are
>   *Judah*, soon to beget royal David,
>   and
>   *Joseph*, constituted by Ephraim and Manasseh,
>   the core tribes of the north.

Father Jacob will not adjudicate between the two,
Judah and Joseph;
>   *His sweeping blessing is for both.*
>   In the long run, Judah will prevail by way of the royal line.

Finished with the task of blessing,

Jacob instructs his sons concerning his burial;
> he is to be planted in the family plot of Abraham in the land of Canaan.

He curled up on his bed.
He breathed his last.
He had done his work.

The text makes no judgment concerning the promissory power of the father;
> but it sees how the father blesses the son,
>> how fathers bless sons,
>> how parents bless their children,
>> how futures are authorized by such promises, and partly not.

This long utterance by old Jacob opens the way for the narrative to come.
> In part, the narrative to follow will perform the promise,
> but not fully.

So it is for us:
> we have been variously blessed and cursed by our parents;
> in powerful ways that legacy shapes us, but not fully.

Even Father Jacob cannot preclude the zone of freedom for his sons.
> His sons live out this legacy,
>> sometimes obediently,
>> sometimes receptively,
>> sometimes willfully,
>> sometimes in gratitude, and
>> sometimes in resentment.

Before long we will come to the imperative of Moses:
> Choose today!

Sons and daughters are always choosing what of the

legacy to embrace;
> our choices are never unencumbered;
>> but they are real choices.
> We exercise elements of freedom but want assurances.
> Like it or not, all the while we are children of the tradition.

We are subject to the impetus of the hidden God.
> It is no wonder that our times are in God's hands, even beyond the destinies of our parents.

We may be grateful for the mix of inheritance and freedom that haunts each of us.

That inheritance works its way amid our freedom;
> our freedom works its way amid the blessing.

The father has left the children with gifts to receive and with tasks to perform.

Where we do not see or know, we may trust and give thanks.

> *We like to think all the siblings in a family are equal. But of course we know better. In many families, there is a designated favorite child. There is a renegade who must make her own way, and there are others who silently accept their assigned roles. You are the God who tips the scale for some and against others. Grant that we may accept your hidden way and that we may mightily protest against savage partiality. We watch the "laying on of hands," and we tremble. Amen.*

ON READING GENESIS 50

"Let the dead bury their own dead;
but as for you, go and proclaim the kingdom of God."
                                            (Luke 9:60)

This final chapter brings closure to the ancestral narrative.
It is preoccupied with the death of Jacob,
> the final chapter in the defining triad of Israel's memory.

Joseph, son of the old man, silently follows the wish of his father.
> The prime minister treats his father to the pageantry of a state funeral in Egyptian fashion,
> with all the honors pertaining thereto.
>> The father discovers, as we all do, that we do not get to plan our own funerals!

The post-funeral time in the family is a liminal moment.
> With the absence of the old sturdy guarantor of order,
> all the old stuff of the family surfaces unsolved.

The brothers, with good reason, are fearful of the retaliation of their brother.
> They remember well enough their maltreatment of him.
> Now he has the power to take vengeance, unrestrained by their father.

Families are like that post-funeral:
> Everything surfaces in that moment, especially old, bad memories.
> Sometimes the old affronts are major . . . like cheating or betrayal.

> Sometimes the old affronts are trivial, like a bad gesture or a careless word.
>
> Sometimes the old affronts remain unidentified, but nonetheless powerful.

The brothers report to Joseph that their father had instructed them to ask forgiveness from him.

> Now, in fearful desperation, they ask:
>
> > Please forgive our sin against you.

They hold their breath:

> Everything depends upon this freighted moment;
>
> > they do not know how their brother will respond to the petition.

The prime minister is either unable or unwilling to utter the word "forgive."

> He does the next best thing:
>
> > he situates the affront of his brothers in a wider context,
> >
> > the context of world famine and his food policy.
> >
> > He dares to say to his brothers:
> >
> > > "You intended evil toward me";
> >
> > yes, you did, no mistake about it.

But — he utters the game-changing adversative;

> but God!

God had a different intention.

God intended good;

> and I, your brother, have done good.

I saved you because God wanted you saved;

> I will provide for you; you can trust my word;
>
> you are safe, and I will keep you safe.
>
> What a sigh of relief!
>
> > They had carried their affront for a long time; and now it is relieved.

It is relieved because of the good faith of their
brother Joseph.
With that good word,
the narrative can move on.
Now the focus is on Joseph;
as always, his case is mixed:
he wants to be buried with his ancestors in
their good land;
but he is embalmed, an Egyptian enterprise;
he never chooses, not even in his death.
This narrative has led me to wonder how it is among us,
at death and post-funeral.
That moment is a time of disorientation,
and potentially of new orientation.
That moment requires
honesty on the part of the brothers, and
generosity on the part of the wounded brother.
Honesty and generosity propel the story forward.
Among us as well, our season of death
requires honesty and generosity,
this in a culture of *fakery* and *parsimony!*
That good work to be done is upstream;
it is hard work, but it is essential.
We may be like the family of Jacob,
capable of more than we knew ahead of time.

We are not unlike Joseph; we carry our beloved dead with us. Sometimes they are a totem of our identity; sometimes they are simply a burden to us. Either way, Joseph moved on. He moved on to face the reality of his brothers. He moved on to enact forgiveness with a promise to provide. Our work at the end of

Genesis is to move on. We may move on with forgiveness for those who have wronged us. Move on with resolve to make provision for the common good. With such good work to do, we may in due course die a peaceable death, with the land of your good promise still in purview. Amen.

CONCLUSION

Beyond the Ancestors

The Genesis narrative—
> the story of the world,
> and the story of the chosen family—
>> prepared the way for the full memory of Israel in song and story.

The fingerprints of this promissory God are all over the exodus narrative:

"God heard their groaning, and God remembered his covenant with *Abraham, Isaac, and Jacob*." (Exod. 2:24)

"He said further, 'I am the God of your fathers, *the God of Abraham, the God of Isaac, and the God of Jacob*.'" (Exod. 3:6)

"Say to them, 'The LORD, the God of your ancestors, *the God of Abraham, of Isaac, and of Jacob*, has appeared to me.'" (v. 16)

". . . so that they may believe that the LORD, the God of their ancestors, *the God of Abraham, the God of Isaac, and the God of Jacob*, has appeared to you." (Exod. 4:5)

"I appeared to *Abraham, Isaac, and Jacob* as God Almighty, but by my name 'The LORD' I did not make myself known to them." (Exod. 6:3)

"I will bring you into the land that I swore to give to *Abraham, Isaac, and Jacob*." (v. 8)

"Remember *Abraham, Isaac, and Israel*, your servants, how you swore to them by your own self." (Exod. 32:13)

"Go, leave this place, you and the people whom you have brought up out of the land of Egypt, and go to the land of which I swore to *Abraham, Isaac, and Jacob*." (Exod. 33:1)

The God of the ancestors is the emancipatory God;
   this God is summoned and mobilized by the cries of the enslaved;
   the enslaved are soon to be Israel;
   for now they are "Hebrews," the lowliest presence in culture.
It is this God who heard,
   who remembered,
      who looked upon, and who noticed.
It is this God who confronted and overpowered Pharaoh;
   now all practices of Egyptian accommodation are terminated.
Miriam invites all of emancipated Israel to sing to this God:
   "Sing to the LORD, for he has triumphed gloriously;
   horse and rider he has thrown into the sea."
      (Exod. 15:21)

The exodus narrative is a one-off.
>It is a nameable event that anchors Israel's emancipatory memory.
>
>Historians are weary with trying to date it.
>>It cannot be dated,
>>
>>because it is always about to happen yet again.

Deep in the exile,
>the great poet of Israel can have God speak in exodus cadences:
>
>"Do not remember the former things,
>>or consider the things of old.
>
>I am about to do a new thing;
>>now it springs forth, do you not perceive it?"
>>>(Isa. 43:18–19)
>
>The exodus is about to happen in Babylon!
>
>The God of the ancestors is about to emancipate again.

Michael Walzer puts it eloquently and wondrously:
First, that wherever you live, it is probably Egypt;
second, that there is a better place, a world more attractive, a promised land;
and third, that "the way to the land is through the wilderness." There is no way to get from here to there except by joining together and marching.[5]

In its singing and in its narratives,
>Israel is always on watch for the new action of the God of the ancestors,
>
>always alert for the keeping of the promises,
>
>always vigilant for the new moment of emancipation.

---

5. Michael Walzer, *Exodus and Revolution* (Baker Books, 1986), 149.

For good reason, the ancestors get extended coverage in the church's recital of the faithful:
- Abraham gets five verses:
  "By faith he received power of procreation, even though he was too old." (Heb. 11:11)
- Isaac gets humble mention:
  "By faith Isaac invoked blessings for the future on Jacob and Esau." (v. 20)
- Jacob gets a verse of mention:
  "By faith Jacob, when dying, blessed each of the sons of Joseph." (v. 21)
- Even Joseph, mostly absent from the styled recitals of faith in Israel, gets a verse:
  "By faith Joseph, at the end of his life, made mention of the exodus of the Israelites and gave instructions about his burial." (v. 22)

These are the faithful who were gladly propelled by the promises of God.

The recital of the faithful who trusted the promises ends on a compelling, poignant contemporary accent:

"Yet all these, though they were commended for their faith, did not receive what was promised, since God had provided something better so that they would not, apart from us, be made perfect." (vv. 39–40)

The recital dares to include us, even us, among the heirs of the promises.

The promises summon and engage us to refuse every easy accommodation,
> to be underway,
>> seeking a good homeland . . .
>>> unashamed!

OTHER PRAYERS ADDRESSED TO THE SAME HOLY LISTENER

A Prayer: You Three Times Holy

The vast company of heaven —
   cherubim, angels, seraphim, archangels —
   gather especially to sing your praises loudly.
      Their constant refrain is,
         "Holy, holy, holy,"
   three times, not more, not less than three.
So we are able to echo their singing as we join in,
         "Holy, holy, holy,"
   three times, not more, not less than three.
We sing that you are ineffable,
        incomprehensible,
          undecodable,
            inaccessible,
              a "tremendous mystery."
In Christian parlance, we take this threefold articulation to match
   our three ways of knowing you to be God.
We say "holy" to the Father,
   the source and ending of all our being,
   you before time, after time, in, with, and under all times,
   Alpha and Omega who loves the world into existence.

It is your will that permits our world to be.
We say "holy" to the Son,
   the one born in a barn,
   the one who had nowhere to lay his head,
     who went about doing good,
       who healed the disabled and restored the disadvantaged,
        who bested empires and the rulers of this age,
         who humbled himself to die on a cross,
          executed as a common criminal,
executed and now risen to authority.
We say "holy" to the Spirit,
   The wind that blew back chaos,
     the force of freedom that made an escape path in the sea;
       the agent of instruction, guidance, and transformation,
       the disturber of our easy peace,
         the one who stirs our lives to new witness and new duty.
We chisel away at your unutterable holiness . . .
   we add modifiers . . .
     love, justice, faithfulness, compassion, steadfastness,
     all true, all good, all important for our life,
but then, yet again, none as thick or daring or bewildering as "holy."
In singing this three times, we acknowledge that you do not fit our categories,
        you do not participate in our equations;
  you do not accommodate our explanatory yearnings.
You three times holy!

Yet you elude us;
> we catch glimpses and yearn to touch and taste and know;
>> and you are there, beyond our control, overwhelming us in awe. Amen.

A Prayer: Your Cosmic Pledge of Disarmament

The report of the flood you caused is not forgotten.
We remember well the torrential rains that swept all before them,
> torrents that swept away so many of your well-beloved creatures.
>> Walls of water overran the good order of your creation.

Your flood lasted so long—
> some said forty days,
> some said 150 days,
>> after so much water, the length of the threat does not matter very much.

We also remember the end of your flood,
> the emergence of dry land,
> the recovery of creaturely life around the world.
>> You uttered your lordly assurance:
>>> that the rhythms of the world would not be disrupted,
>>>> we could count on
>>>>> summer and winter,
>>>>> cold and heat,
>>>>> seedtime and harvest,
>>>>> day and night.

Beyond that, we remember your attentive gesture of assurance:
> The appearance of a rainbow;
>> you hung up your bow;
>>> you retired your weapon;
>>>> you engaged in disarmament,
>>>>> signaling the end of hostility between you and your creation.

In that moment of your disarmament,
> you decided you would govern in a "more excellent way,"
>> by the generosity of love,
>> by the reliability of restorative justice,
>> by the lavishness of your forgiveness.

You would not govern by fear;
> rather you would run the endless risk of the excellent way of self-giving.

We see your more excellent way all through your history:
> We see it in the exodus and your solidarity with the enslaved;
>
> we smell it in the manna bread of wilderness;
>
> we know it in the pathos of the prophets.
>> Finally, we see your self-giving agency embodied in Jesus of Nazareth,
>>
>> who required his own leader to put up his sword, yet more disarmament.

The savagery goes on
> amid the predatory superpowers,
>
> amid the brutal struggles for territory and resources,
>
> amid our ignoble disputes with our neighbors.

Your weapon has been retired and suspended in midair for a long time,
> lingering for us to decode its meaning.

You have renounced violent ways.

Peace indeed!

Peace not "beginning with me,"
> but with the Lord of the flood.

We are awed by new possibilities. Amen.

A Prayer: You with the Long Nose

Among the best-loved and most-often-reiterated recitals concerning you is first on the lips of Moses:
"The LORD, the LORD,
a God merciful and gracious,
slow to anger,
and abounding in steadfast love and faithfulness,
keeping steadfast love for the thousandth generation,
forgiving iniquity and transgression and sin."
(Exod. 34:6–7)
This often-repeated formula witnesses your eager solidarity with us and with your entire creation.
Among the reassuring terms of your recital is the phrase "slow to anger."
The phrase is a flat, uninspired translation of a compelling phrase in Hebrew,
a phrase declaring you, our well-beloved God, to have long nostrils,
a long nose.
Your long nose requires you to inhale and exhale at great length to renew your breath.
You are, sometimes, the God who breathes the fire of anger and indignation,
and we can imagine a flow of fire from your nose.
Except that your nostrils are long;
the fire cools,
the anger subsides,
the indignation wanes.
By the time your flame of rage reaches outside your nose,
it has cooled.
It has cooled so that you can recover your balance.

It has cooled enough for you to reassert your long-running resolve to be
> a God who practices steadfast love and faithfulness.

We are glad for your long nose.
We are glad for your cooling nostrils.
We are grateful that the rage and indignation do not last,
> not for long,
> not through the night,
> not into the next day.
>> We are thankful that we know you at your best,
>> > free from anger beyond a short temper,
>> > > patient even with our recurring waywardness.

The myths are filled with tales concerning gods who manipulate and goddesses who deceive;
but you are not like that:
> You are not underhanded or secretive in your governance;
> > you are your own true self every time;

You are a reliable presence in our common life.
You move among us with equilibrium and great resolve on our behalf.
> And we are on the receiving end of the breath of life you give.

In our inhaling we become capable of generous fidelity.
Your long nose of fire is but a mere footnote to your long, life-giving commitment to the world that you love.
It turns out that we—not unlike you—are capable of forgiveness when we have cooled from our indignation.
Move in and through our anger, cooling us enough to participate in your life-giving breath.

We are grateful that we may be alongside you as we cool enough to care in generative ways. Move us past our hot noses to do the good work cooled noses make possible. Amen.

A Prayer: Fresh from the Word
(On Reading Isaiah 55:10–13)

At the outset, there was the silence of despair.
And then You spoke:
   You said, "Let there be light."
   You said, "Let my people go."
   You said, "Comfort, comfort my people."
Your word became flesh before our very eyes:
   Light became creation;
   Emancipation became covenant people;
   Comfort became homecoming.
     Your word is not empty, but full of futures.
You said, "Love God," and we are summoned.
You said, "Love neighbor," and we are implicated.
You said, "Follow me," and we are on a different way with you.
   Your word, in its life-giving power, addresses us every day.
   Your word, in its life-dispatching force, empowers us every day.
   Your word, in its restorative passion, makes new every day.
We are creatures of your word;
   we cannot be otherwise;
   we would not choose to be otherwise.
It is because of your faithful word that we are on our way . . . rejoicing;
on our way in freedom, mercy, compassion, and justice,
on our way to neighborly well-being,
on our way rejoicing. Amen.

www.ingramcontent.com/pod-product-compliance
Lightning Source LLC
Chambersburg PA
CBHW020051210126
38509CB00001B/1